S.C   E
tr   stories

Look-in

Also available
in this series:

PONIES AND YOU
Sue Turner

THE WILD WEST
Robin May

IS THERE LIFE IN OUTER SPACE?
Peter Fairley

EXPLORING WOODS
Peter Schofield

HAVE FUN WITH ORIGAMI
Robert Harbin

S.O.S. WILDLIFE

true Survival stories

VICTOR EDWARDS

illustrated by
Peter Kesterman

From the famous Television series

Look-in
Independent Television Books Limited, London

INDEPENDENT TELEVISION BOOKS LTD.
247 Tottenham Court Road
London W1P 0AU

ISBN 0 900 72727 6

Printed in Great Britain by
Tinling (1973) Ltd, Prescot, Merseyside
(a member of the Oxley Printing Group)

CONTENTS

Introduction 6
1 Wildlife in London 7
2 Pelican Flyway 13
3 The Flight of the Snow Geese 19
4 Citizens of the Coral 30
5 Where Him of the Hairy Hands lives 35
6 The World of the Beaver 39
7 The Trout and the Mayfly 45
8 The World you never see 53
9 The Forbidden Desert of the Danakil 58
10 The Empty Desert 65
11 The Loneliest Place in the World 72
12 Deathtrap Lake 78
13 S O S Rhino 82
14 First Catch Your Unicorn 88
15 Wings over the Rift 95
16 The Family that lived with Elephants 101
17 The Enchanted Isles 112
18 Now or Never 120
19 What makes a Wildlife Cameraman 121
Acknowledgements 128

INTRODUCTION

Can you imagine a world without lions, tigers, elephants, bears and hundreds of other interesting and beautiful animals? It could happen and once a species is wiped out nothing can ever bring it back.

Why are some animals battling to survive while others don't have to? Many *wild* animals, living in a wild state, are now in danger because man is not only occupying more and more space in the world but he is polluting and destroying the areas that remain truly wild. Wild animals are being pushed out. In many cases they can continue to survive only where they are given special protected areas such as reserves and national parks. This is true of big cats such as the leopard, cheetah, tiger and jaguar, and the largest mammals such as the polar bear, elephant and rhino.

Sophisticated killing methods can take a heavy toll. You would think that the polar bear, living in the Arctic region virtually uninhabited by man, would be safe, but visitors to those regions now hunt the bear from aircraft and helicopters.

Of course, domestic animals are in no danger. There is no shortage of dogs and cats for pets, or of farm animals that provide food, such as sheep, cows, chickens and pigs. There is surely a lesson here that can help us to preserve wildlife.

Man must learn — he is slowly discovering the fact — that wildlife is essential to his happiness and welfare. It is essential for several reasons. Because the presence of wild animals in the wild places of the world is a sure indication that we are keeping at least some of our planet clean and healthy. Because wildlife is beautiful and is one of the joys man is entitled to experience on this earth. Because wildlife can add to man's prosperity — as African countries have found by attracting millions of tourists each year to their national parks.

Man is responsible for safe-guarding the world's remaining wildlife and he must learn everything there is to know about the creatures in order to preserve them.

Not all the stories in this book are about creatures threatened by man. Some are stories of how creatures survive in the wild state in the face of natural competition from climate and predators. Other stories are about man himself and how he survives in extreme climatic conditions. For man, never forget, is an animal too, but, he is a thinking animal and it is this ability to think that sets him apart and gives him a special responsibility towards the other animal inhabitants of Planet Earth.

1
WILDLIFE IN LONDON

A blurred shape moves silently across a darkening summer sky in a London square. The tawny owl, on the hunt for mice, long after other birds have gone to roost, can still be heard making its haunting call in central London as the roar of the traffic quietens at night. Wildlife is much more adaptable to big city life than we imagine. We think of kestrels and owls as creatures of the open countryside and deep forest, yet we know they also prey on mice, young pigeons and sparrows in London parks and squares.

Over the years, kestrels have nested in the most unexpected places — a shaft in a power station at Greenwich and at the Palace of Westminster, for instance. One pair nested on the sixteenth floor of a block of flats in the Old Kent Road. They chose an empty window box and inside the adjoining room was a television set. The noise, the lights, the nearness of people didn't bother them. They successfully hatched out four young in their window box. During that time the male bird was busy preying on house mice or an occasional young pigeon or sparrow to feed his young family. By noon every day the ledge on which they nested was out of the sun. Only in the early morning did the mother have to shade her chicks.

We do not know what brings kestrels to nest and hunt in London in preference to cliffs or the tall trees of the country Possibly it's the plentiful supply of food with little competition from others of their kind. And have you ever wondered what the city of London must look like to a soaring kestrel? The tall buildings must give them a sense of being among steep, rocky canyons. Once the birds have adapted to the noise and the people, there are plenty of handy nesting ledges about, as well as a good food supply.

Think of the sprawl of London, the amount of food concentrated within its area and the opportunities there are for birds of all kinds to nest and feed in the square kilometres of buildings, warehouses, shrubs, trees, parkland, commons, water reservoirs, gravel pits, sewage farms, rivers, lakes, ponds, orchards and gardens, rubbish tips, factories, power stations — the list is almost endless.

There are three cockney characters you will never have any trouble spotting in London — the pigeon, the sparrow and the starling. Tame London pigeons as well as wild wood pigeons strut about the place as though they owned it. As for starlings, millions of them take over the fun spots of London, like Leicester Square and Trafalgar Square, as a roost in the autumn and winter. As the weather gets colder, they move in from parks and outlying districts at sunset to the warmth and bright lights. Before they settle for the night they wheel round in huge flocks and chatter incessantly as they take up every centimetre of roof, ledge and tree space in their thousands.

But London is rich in many other birds, which form a changing pattern throughout the year as migrants come and go. Pied wagtails, herons, blackbirds, missel thrushes, wood pigeons, the timid jay and tree creeper all nest in London squares and some parks; late in the year, fieldfares and redwings fly in from their summer nesting grounds in Scandinavia. Other migrants are the cuckoo, swift, swallow, skylark, whinchat, chiff chaff, common sandpiper and yel-

Kestrel and young

Black-headed gulls in St. James's Park

low wagtail. The best places to see these birds are Kensington Gardens, Hyde Park, Regent's Park, St James's Park, Battersea Park, Hampstead Heath, Wimbledon Common.

London is equally rich in water birds. The river Thames attracts a great variety. It's a broad flyway, a kind of birds' M1 for migrants from Iceland, Greenland, Siberia, Scandinavia and all the countries of Europe. If you see black-headed gulls flying up river from the sea you can be sure that autumn is near. Some have spent the summer in nesting colonies down at the coast, some have flown from Scandinavia and the Baltic to be with us. Like wealthy tourists, they will be spending the cold winter months in the comparative mildness of London in the parks and by the riverside.

The unexpected will always happen in London. Cormorants, skuas and guillemots have all been seen on rare occasions and, many years ago, a puffin landed in the middle of the Strand, stopping the traffic. St James's Park is one of the showplaces of central London for water birds It isn't surprising. When the winter gales blow wildfowl in from the Thames estuary and they follow the line of the river, they see the glint of water from the park lake, a lake that King Charles II created to accommodate his own collection of water birds. There are tame ducks and geese there now. Many have their wings clipped to prevent their flying north when spring comes round. But there are many more wild ducks, mallard and tufted, free to come and go. Once, a tufted duck, ringed at St James's in May, turned up in Siberia in September, a flight of 4,000 kilometres.

Other important sources of bird life are London's big reservoirs. At the Walthamstow reservoirs in east London, which teem with fish, herons build their untidy nests in the tall trees on an island. Here, too, great crested grebes put on their courtship display every spring, a ritual dance that includes the offering of gifts in the form of water weed. And in winter at Barn Elms reservoir in Hammersmith, wigeon, many from Russia, mix with coot and tufted duck.

The bird population of a city like London changes all the time as conditions in the city itself change. For instance, after the last war the bombed and empty sites attracted quite a rare bird to nest in London, the black redstart. Now that these sites have been built on, the bird doesn't nest in the city any more. But as London loses one species it gains

Ducks in St. James's Park

another. Cleaner air, due to a ban on coal fires in central London, has brought back nesting colonies of house martins. The insects the martins need for feeding their young have returned because they thrive in clean air.

Things are certainly improving for birds in London. There is evidence, based on observation by bird watchers, that in the past fifty years many species have adapted themselves to living in a man-made environment of bricks and concrete.

Among mammals, too, London has its regulars. The wily old fox is remarkable. There are foxes around Hampstead Heath and Wimbledon that raid dustbins at night and they have been seen slinking across London gardens in the early mornings. Only a few months ago, foxes decimated a collection of Chinese water deer, cranes and wallabies in the gardens of the Horniman Museum near Dulwich.

The fox is cunning, determined and adaptable. Traffic, noise, lights, people, shooting, trapping and hunting — nothing, it seems, will stop the London fox. It feeds on mice, rats, small birds and scraps of food left in gardens overnight. Where does a London fox live in daytime? It makes its earth, the hole in which it lives, in rubbish dumps, waste ground and especially railway embankments.

Suburban fox

On the outskirts of London, in places like Wimbledon Common and Epping Forest, a wide range of mammals thrives, not only stoats and weasels but badgers and, in Epping, wild fallow deer. As to rabbits, they cling on in allotments and nursery farms around London that have never been ravaged by the deadly rabbit plague, myxomatosis. Hares thrive in the large areas of grass around the runways of London airport at Heathrow, as does the little gamebird, the ptarmigan.

Grey squirrels hardly need pointing out in gardens and parks all over London. The grey squirrel, introduced from America in the last century, feeds on acorns, fir cones, small buds, bulbs, roots, soft fruit and fungus and it is blamed for the decline of the red squirrel. It builds its nest — called a drey — of twigs lined with moss and grass in the fork of a tree.

One animal we are never likely to lose in London is the brown or Norway rat. Within the sewers, rubbish tips, warehouses and the foundations of big buildings it can easily make itself at home, gnawing its way to any handy food supply. In the docks area of London the black rat or ship rat lives and feeds. This one is a great climber and a good swimmer and, unlike the brown rat, which will nest underground, it will often build its nest behind rafters or pipes in a roof.

Above water is fine for the birds. But what about *in* the water of the Thames? Can any fish survive in its polluted water? Two hundred years ago, the Thames was a notable salmon river. The last salmon was caught at Richmond in 1833. Alas, the Thames anglers have never again felt the tug of a fighting salmon.

Yet there are signs that the river is getting cleaner. Not so long ago, a fishing match was organised on a stretch of the river between Battersea power station and Hammersmith bridge and the anglers actually hooked live fish. They caught bleak — a fish only a few centimetres long. But the important thing is that the bleak likes reasonably clean water, so it seems there is every chance, if the Thames continues to get cleaner, that other fish will be able to live there.

2
PELICAN FLYWAY

Sixteen kilometres out in Lake Shala, in the Rift Valley of Ethiopia, there is a one hectare island almost constantly veiled by heat haze. There are no boats on the lake because there are no fish of any size in its sodary waters. So the island is never visited by Africans. It is completely free from disturbance. Nor is the lake one on which anyone would want to boat for pleasure. Fierce squalls suddenly sweep across it from the surrounding mountains. The sun's rays reflect from the water as through a burning glass. Shala is 1,820 metres above sea level and the ultraviolet light has a severe burning effect in the slightly rarefied air.

Until recently the island I have described was a mystery island, too inhospitable to be visited by man. Then two

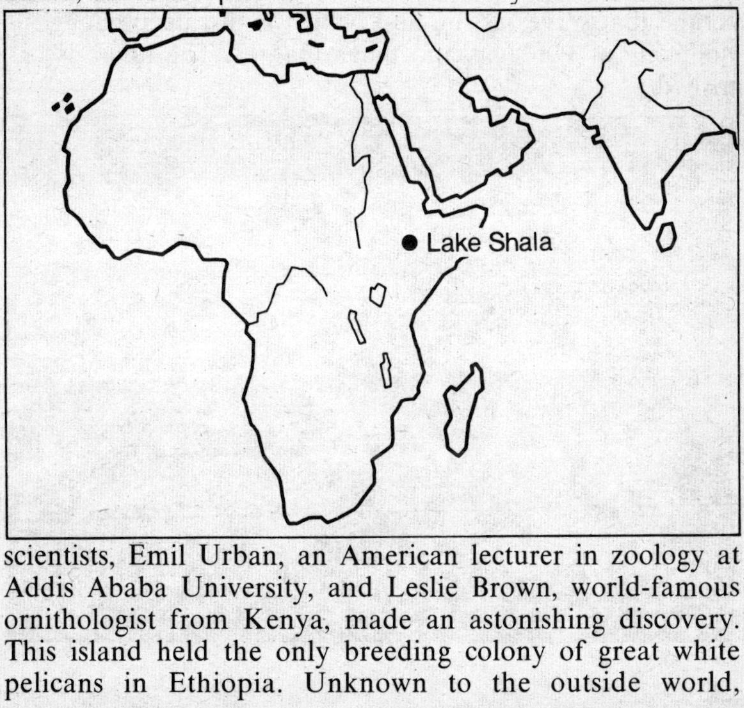

scientists, Emil Urban, an American lecturer in zoology at Addis Ababa University, and Leslie Brown, world-famous ornithologist from Kenya, made an astonishing discovery. This island held the only breeding colony of great white pelicans in Ethiopia. Unknown to the outside world, thousands of pelicans had been nesting there for centuries. Up to 5,000 nesting pairs were packed on to this one hectare. Urban and Brown counted 2,000 pairs nesting in an area only 45 metres square.

Until then no one had any idea where the vast great pelican population of the northern half of the Rift Valley nested. At last the mystery was solved. The pelicans had chosen this lonely little island because it gave them complete security from human interference.

From the first trip across the stormy lake the scientists were careful not to disturb the nesting birds, creeping up behind a ridge of volcanic lava to remain unseen. Later on, they built a permanent hide.

With great white pelicans, home building comes only after mating. The collecting of nesting material is done by the male alone. He scoops out a hollow in the ground with his big beak, collects odd bits of twigs and grass and presents them to his mate. She arranges them in the shallow scrape that serves as the nest, which is just deep enough to hold one or two eggs and that's that. . . . The home is furnished.

Great white pelicans

Considering their size and weight — an adult pelican has a wing span of almost three metres and weighs up to 11 kilos — they are pretty careful where they put their feet. Few eggs in the overcrowded colony get cracked and the females often use their great webbed feet to cover the egg in order to incubate it. A remote island like this protects the colony from four-footed predators, but it can't stop raiding birds, such as the kite, the Egyptian vulture and the fish eagle, from trying to snatch an egg or a chick. The pelican, however, doesn't panic. Colonies of some birds try to defend their nests against intruders with the result that everything becomes disorganised, which is exactly what an intruder wants. But pelicans sit tight on their eggs when the raiders are about. They seem to know, instinctively, that this is the most sensible course.

When the chicks hatch out they are pink and downy. At about a week old they turn jet black. They are fed on a kind of watered fish soup, pre-digested. The parent makes its young stick its head inside its pouch to feed.

The discovery of this pelican island in the lake was startling enough. But now an intriguing question presented itself. Shala could not possibly support big fish-eaters like the pelicans. The colony needed two tonnes of fish a day. During the five-month nesting season that means 300 tonnes of fish. Where did the pelicans catch them?

After weeks of watching, Emil Urban and Leslie Brown pieced together the whole fantastic story. It begins at about ten o'clock every morning when squadrons of pelicans begin to get airborne. First, they fly three or four kilometres out into the lake, alight on the water and wait, forming themselves into groups of twenty or thirty. A few kilometres across the water on Shala's northern shore is a 914 metre-high mountain that separates Shala from another lake, called Abiata, 24 kilometres away. Abiata is full of fish. But before the pelicans can get at Abiata's fish they've got to climb 914 metres to fly over that mountain. To attempt to do so by flapping their wings would not only be extremely wasteful of energy, it would probably prove beyond their power. But pelicans, for all their weight, are magnificent gliders. Their broad wings enable them to soar like a sailplane. So they sit on the surface of Shala in waiting squadrons on the look-out for a thermal — a fast-rising current of warm air. Soon, conditions are right. Dust devils begin to whirl indicating thermals on the far shore and, as the morning becomes warmer, the first formations take off. From now on they will take off at, roughly, twenty-minute intervals. They spiral up as if on a giant aerial escalator. Sometimes, apparently for the pure joy of it, they continue soaring until they are 3,000 metres above sea level. Once over the peak of the mountain, their target, Abiata, comes into view. This is where the pelicans will spend the next twenty-four hours, each catching two or three kilos of fish.

They seldom seem to land in mass formation and never where they intend to feed. They either touch down in ones or twos or land far out in the lake and paddle in to the feeding area, a small flooded wood of acacia trees where streams flow into the lake attracting large shoals of fish. Great white pelicans fish together, dipping their heads in unison like a team of rowers bending to the oars. Sometimes they form a circle to surround the fish and to drive the shoals into the shallows where they can be easily picked off. When you watch them you can see that only a handful in each party are successful at each dip of the bill. The lucky ones throw back their heads to swallow the fish, usually a *Tilapia,* to be held in their pouch.

Once they have caught their load of fish the pelicans spend a great deal of time and care in preening. It's rather like servicing an airliner. Flight feathers must be in tip-top condition for the flight home to the hungry chicks left behind on Lake Shala. Now, of course, they have to find a thermal to carry them back over the mountain.

When they touch down on the home island, the chicks immediately spot their own parents. The well-grown young are made to chase them, begging for food, ravenously hungry. It's a kind of training for the time (soon to come) when they will have to find their own food. It's a pelican riot. Pushing into the parent's capacious pouch, the young chick scoops out the pre-digested fish.

So the young grow and learn to fly, but only a few of

them will follow their parents to Lake Abiata. Once they become competent flyers, the young simply take off and vanish from the island. No one, not even Emil Urban or Leslie Brown who unravelled this story, knows exactly where they go for the first year or two of their lives. What we do know is that when they are three years old some magical instinct, some powerful race memory, pulls them back to the island in Lake Shala to raise *their* families.

Filming the story of Lake Shala's pelicans set Dieter Plage plenty of problems. One of the hardest to solve was how to get close enough to swimming pelicans to film them from water level. When he swam out to the pelicans clad in a wet suit and using a camera in an underwater housing, he found he couldn't get within half a kilometre of them. Suspicious, they simply swam away, far out of camera range. But because he wanted close-ups he knew he had to think of some plan to get close to these elusive birds.

The answer came on a visit to Dr Urban at the University in Addis Ababa. Urban showed him a stuffed pelican and

Dieter's decoy

suggested a decoy might be the answer. Dieter gladly made a donation towards the upkeep of the museum there and took the stuffed pelican away wrapped up in newspaper.

On the island, Dieter hollowed out the stuffed carcase of the bird, put the camera inside so that the lens looked out through a hole just below the long neck and left just enough space to get his head inside as well. Then he swam out to the birds with the dummy supported on an inflated motor tyre. The plan worked. So far as the pelicans of Lake Shala were concerned, Dieter was just another one of them. He went so close that some of them touched him. Young ones even came up to be fed. 'In fact, one chick followed me all the time, followed me when I had finished filming for the day, and stayed with the dummy pelican on the beach.'

But there was a price to pay for the success. Dieter spent fifty hours all told in the water. Even though he wore a wet suit, the sodary waters of Shala removed most of the skin from his body, just like a very bad case of sunburn.

3
THE FLIGHT OF THE SNOW GEESE

Three hundred thousand snow geese nest and breed on the tundra to the west of Hudson Bay in Canada during the short Arctic summer and then, with winter closing in on them, they fly south to Texas and the Mississippi delta. By the following April the flocks are moving north once again to nest and breed. From time immemorial this pattern of the snow geese swinging backwards and forwards across the vast North American continent in a migration rhythm of feeding and breeding has been one of the wonders of the world. The length of their migration route is some 4,000 kilometres and the *Survival* film team of Des and Jen Bartlett covered every kilometre of it.

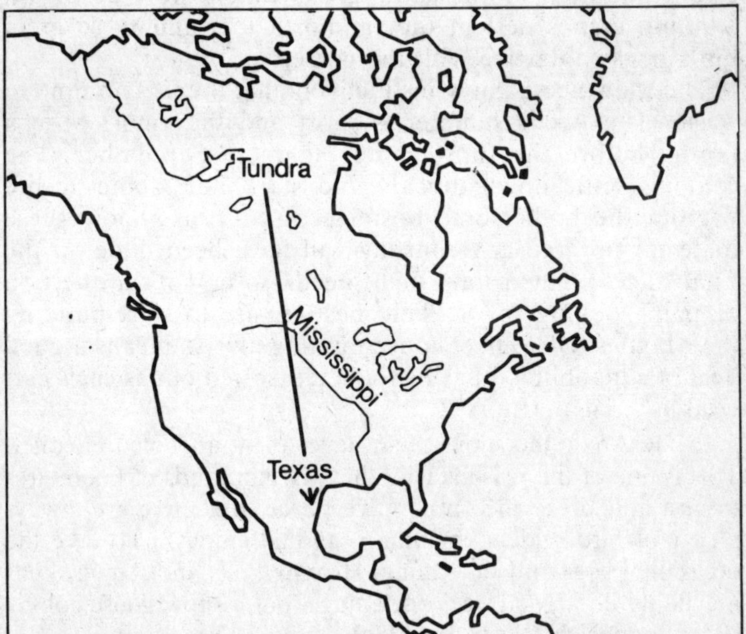

When they arrived at the McConnell river delta to the west of Hudson Bay in northern Canada in mid-May to begin filming the snow geese on their nesting ground, a reluctant spring had not yet arrived. Nor had the geese. They set up camp on the snow-covered and still frozen ground in a treeless waste of numbing cold and sudden blizzards. As the snow melted on the tundra, as these Arctic wastes are called, the snow geese began to arrive, the first flocks flying overhead, moving still further north. A week later the flocks were increasing in size, and at mid-morning on 23 May the Bartletts estimated three hundred an hour; two days later the snow geese were flying overhead in V-shaped formations, giving their haunting calls, all day long.

By now the ice was breaking up in the McConnell river. The landscape was still dappled with patches of snow and the days were warm but deceptive because at night it froze again. The snow geese kept coming and with them a good many blue geese, which are not a separate species but a colour variation of the snow goose called the blue phase. Sandhill cranes nest in the far north too, and these great birds began to arrive with the geese.

The snow geese know instinctively that there is no time to waste. The Arctic summer is short and they must raise a family before the snow comes again in September. The colonies settle down quickly and start their domestic life without the bothersome business of courting. Snow geese mate for life and any courting will have been done on the final stages of their long flight north, so now it's a question of pairs looking for a likely nesting site to start building their homes. Of course, house hunting always means a good deal of squabbling, but this soon gets sorted out as each pair establishes its territory.

In the Arctic the snow geese have few four-footed enemies. This is one of the reasons why they fly thousands of kilometres to nest and breed in comparative peace. But there are always plenty of bird raiders, including sandhill cranes, who take the occasional eggs and the young. Herring gulls and Arctic skuas inevitably do a good deal of damage, but a snow goose colony is large enough to survive all these hazards.

Each female broods an average of about five eggs in just over three weeks. The goslings hatch out pretty much together and are active from the start. They leave the nest the moment they are hatched and the parents take the youngsters out on to open ground towards the river. They are swimming and feeding almost immediately. Flying lessons come later.

In the centre of all this activity Des and Jen Bartlett lived and worked in often severe conditions; there were wind gusts close to 80 kilometres per hour and steady gales blew across the unprotected and bleak 3-kilometre-wide delta of the McConnell river. They made long tramps across the boggy tundra carrying 22-kilo packs and film gear to their filming locations.

But their reward came in the form of many unique incidents never before captured on film, including a battle between two devoted snow goose parents and a pair of sandhill cranes, into whose nesting territory the geese had led their young family. One of the cranes actually seized a

Snow goose and goslings

gosling but then dropped it when the parents attacked, so that the snow goose chick escaped without harm.

One of the highlights of the Bartletts' stay on the tundra was when they found themselves, almost accidentally, adopting young birds abandoned by their parents. It often happens that a few goslings wander away from the nest right after hatching. The parents go off without them so they get separated from the family. Sometimes a chick hatches out after the rest of the family have left, and so becomes easy prey for the skuas or herring gulls. Des and Jen saw quite a bit of this and felt so sorry they set about rescuing about a dozen strays and late hatchers. And soon they became the goslings' 'parents'.

One of the fascinating things about orphaned goslings is that they quickly attach themselves to people. Movement and human speech seem to attract them. They gradually become convinced that the humans are their real parents. Scientists call this process 'imprinting'. The goslings followed the Bartletts everywhere, chattering away and trying to help with whatever they were doing. Oddly enough they

Adopted goslings 'helping' Jen with the washing

even got along with a previously adopted orphan, a young sandhill crane the Bartletts had named Fred.

By August the goslings had grown rapidly. They were always tugging at the guy ropes of the Bartletts' tent or picking mosquitoes off their legs. The Bartletts, as foster parents, had to take the chicks everywhere and were followed by them for kilometres across the tundra when they set out to film. By mid-August the orphans were fully qualified fliers and this new-won ability freed them from serious concern for predators. They could take to the air now if they were threatened. However, they did cause one serious problem, a problem that the sandhill crane, Fred, helped to solve. Des Bartlett described it in a letter:

'We've lost a lot of sleep recently with the flapping of the tents in the wind. What has kept us awake even more, however, has been an unnerving night visitor. We can now honestly say that we have been within a foot of a wild polar bear.

'We had just finished dinner when Fred, our sandhill crane, gave his alarm call. The polar bear was about thirty metres away, sniffing the air appreciatively. He could probably smell our adopted snow geese. He was still in the willows two hundred metres out when we went to bed, so we put the geese in an old army hut here. It leaks in dozens of places but it was safer than the tent.

'Two chaps from Guelph University had planned to visit us (Bob and Dave) but as they had not turned up we thought they had changed their plans. However, we had not been in our sleeping bags long before they arrived. Getting dressed in this climate is quite a hassle, so we stayed put and told them about the bear. They took the steaks they had brought with them and went to cook outside the hut.

'Soon, Fred was giving his alarm call and we knew the bear was back. It walked up to the side of the hut just as Bob looked round the corner. Great excitement. . . shouts and arm waving by Bob and Dave, but no panic on the part of the bear — it really wanted those steaks. It went behind the hut and the chaps naturally looked round the other side for it, but it doubled back and gave them a nasty start from behind. They must have brought an arsenal with them as thunderflashes (explosive fireworks) started going off all over the place. Then Dave started using flares fired from a shotgun and the bear ran off.

'As you can imagine, it was not too easy to get back to sleep after all that excitement. Every flap of the tent, was the bear back again. . . or was it? However, we must have dropped off as the bear did wake us up around one a.m. His dark silhouette loomed large over our heads on the canvas tent wall only thirty centimetres away. He was shaking and ripping the tent as he tried to push in through the narrow opening. As we had no firecrackers we could only shout to scare the bear. I thought I shouted so loud it would wake the dead, but it did not panic the bear. . . .

'At last, the bear backed out of the hole and slowly walked along the side of the tent, his outline showing clearly as a dark shadow on the canvas. We yelled again and he carried on his merry way. Once his shadow left the tent we had no means of knowing where he was. His big feet made no sound on the mossy tundra. Later, Jen and I both remarked on his snuffling breathing: it was the only sound we heard from him.'

One day in September a biting wind blew from the north. It was the first hint to the geese that it was time to go south. Year after year the geese that nest around Hudson Bay follow the same route. It's called the 'central flyway' and it reaches down into the United States through North and South Dakota to Oklahoma, Texas and the Gulf of Mexico. All down the flyway are refuges set up by U.S. conservation authorities to feed the migrating birds. They could be described as stepping stones for the geese on this long flight.

The wild geese would fly south as they always did, but what about the orphans? They would have to go with the Bartletts when they packed up to follow the flight of the snow geese south. There seemed to be nothing else to do but take them on their first migration, as their true parents would have done.

It's 1,600 kilometres from Hudson Bay to the U.S. border, and when the Bartletts arrived there with the goslings in a specially built trailer the U.S. customs men looked up their book of regulations and said, in effect, 'you can't import

U.S. Customs meet the geese

those geese through here.' Des pointed out the wild skeins (a flock of geese in flight) that were right then flying across the border over their heads. The customs men said ah, yes, *they* were airborne and the customs have no control over wild geese. Des said he could get his adopted goslings airborne — would that be all right? The customs men raised no objection; in fact they stopped all the traffic while Des let the geese out of the truck on to the road. They took off, wheeled round and then headed north, back to Canada! The customs men watched them vanish and let the Bartletts through. Des drove a few hundred metres on to the American soil of North Dakota and waited. Sure enough, his orphaned geese gradually swung in a wide circle and flew over the border to land by the stationary truck.

Sand Lake Refuge, South Dakota, is the first stopping place for the snow geese after they have crossed the Canadian-American border. It's a staggering sight to see thousands upon thousands of geese — sometimes as many as 200,000 in a single flock — planing down on the lakes and the specially planted corn fields that are provided for them. Against the red and yellow autumn tints of the trees they look like a dense white snowfall as they settle. You can

'Clark Gable' posing for the camera

A passing visitor on the Tundra

Snowgeese in flight

Snow geese defending young against attack by sandhill cranes

stand at night when the full moon rises and watch them flying, silhouetted against its pale disc. Snow geese are fine night flyers, navigating by the moon and stars. They stay feeding at Sand Lake until the first snow flurries tell them it is time to move south again.

Some make for the De Soto Refuge on the borders of Iowa and Nebraska while others, impelled by the first snow covering the farmlands below them as they fly, push on further to Squaw Creek, Missouri. But along the flyway, on the perimeters of the refuges, the licensed hunters wait with guns. It's a gauntlet that the snow geese run every year and along the flyway some 50,000 of them will die. The United States Fish and Wildlife Service say that the geese population can stand this sort of loss without serious inroads being made. The geese hunters' licence fees are all spent on research and conservation of the geese.

By the end of April the foster goslings were all but full grown with one or two strong leaders in their group. They were approaching the time when family ties normally break down. In many ways they were already living free. They had not been caged from the beginning. They would often fly a few kilometres out of sight, or join the wild flocks for a few hours, and there was no way the Bartletts could get them back. It was always up to the geese whether they returned or not.

Once, when the Bartletts visited De Soto Refuge in Missouri, they lost a goose — temporarily. It was the one they called Clark Gable because, somehow, it was always *his* face that was in front of the camera. One windy day he joined the wild flocks and didn't return. They searched and searched but how could they find a young goose among an estimated 300,000 of them on the refuge?

Two days later, however, one of the refuge workmen operating a grader on a back road saw a young, lone snow goose that did not fly away. He was able to walk right up to it, pick it up and bring it back to Des and Jen in his truck. It was Clark Gable with a small pellet wound on its breast under the left wing. He was really pleased to be back.

When the migrant flocks reach Texas and the Gulf of Mexico they find rice fields, grain, and sweet short grass as well as coastal marshes on which to feed. Among them are many young birds who have been led all the way from northern Canada to Texas by their parents, for geese learn the migration route purely by following their parents.

By March there is a charged, restless atmosphere among the wild flocks. They feel the north wind pulling at their instincts with the urge to nest and breed. They become more and more clamorous, as though they are talking about the journey north they have to make. This instinctive, natural drive to breed was as strong in the adopted goslings as it was in the wild flocks and it was in May that the Bartletts saw the last of their flock.

Des describes his last sight of their geese. 'The youngsters had been getting more and more excitable and talkative. A few days ago they were on the wing as they often are. They rose and circled around us, getting further and further away each time they circled, until their little skein faded into the blue sky. They haven't come back this time.'

The Bartletts didn't see them again. They had returned to the wild of their own free will.

4
CITIZENS OF THE CORAL

When Italy entered the Second World War on the side of Nazi Germany against the Allies, which included Britain and France, there were thousands of Italian soldiers in East Africa. To supply this army, Italy despatched an ammunition ship loaded with bombs, land mines and shells to Massawa, a port on the Red Sea. The ship, named the *Umbria,* never reached Massawa. On the day Italy declared war the *Umbria* was caught by a British warship north of Suakin, offshore from Port Sudan, and the Italian captain scuttled his ship rather than allow the cargo of explosives to fall into enemy hands. The *Umbria* went down on the Wingate reef where she lies today.

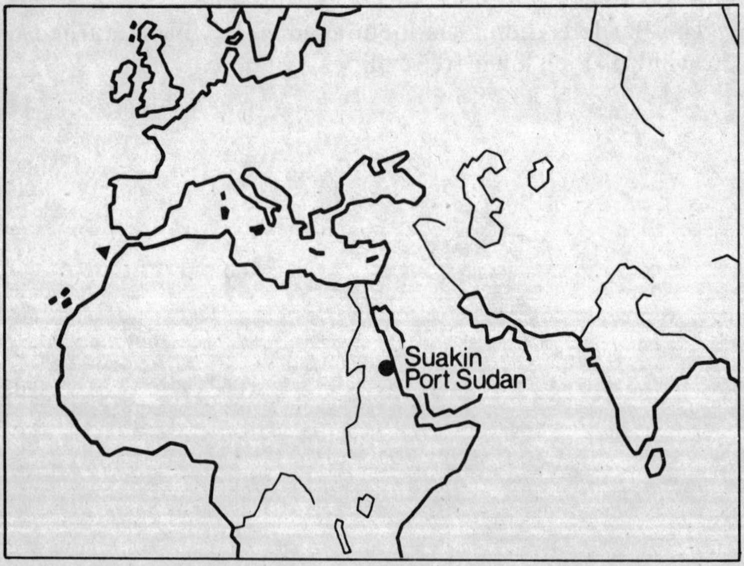

Suakin's harbour was once filled with British troop transports and cargo ships, but over the years nature has changed all this. Slowly, inexorably, the port of Suakin has been strangled by a coral reef that has completely closed the harbour to big ships.

Coral is the work of millions of tiny, communal creatures called polyps. Most of them secrete a rock-like defensive crust around their soft bodies, hence the coral reefs. The shores of the Red Sea are bordered by coral reefs and the Wingate reef is just one of these. Sunken ships are quickly colonised by coral in the Red Sea and the *Umbria* was no exception.

But those tons of rusted explosives lying in the holds of the *Umbria* are still a force to be reckoned with. Extremely sensitive and highly dangerous, the whole lot could explode at any time, shattering the coral wreck and rocking modern Port Sudan, as well as the ancient town of Suakin. A *Survival* team led by Dieter Plage, set out to film the *Umbria.*

Sir Peter Scott, *Survival's* scientific advisor, has explored reefs all over the world. He rates our knowledge of reef fish today at about the same standard as the knowledge of birds in the eighteenth century before the invention of binoculars. He argues that the invention of scuba diving gear will produce the same breakthrough because scientists and naturalists can now watch reef fish at close quarters and observe their behaviour. There are many scientific discoveries waiting to be made just by watching.

Sponge coral

Among the many interesting fish found around the *Umbria* is the Amphiprion, which likes to shelter in the arms of a killer. Sometimes known as the clownfish, because of its bright markings, it benefits from its relationship with the killer — the sea anemone — which has poisonous tentacles. (The sea anemone is an animal and not a plant as its name wrongly implies.) The clownfish receives protection from predators and, possibly, gets food scraps left over from the anemone's victims. How does the clownfish do this without being killed?

Peter Scott explains: 'To save confusion, each tentacle of the sea anemone secretes a chemical that tells the other tentacles that it is one of them and not to be stung and eaten. The clownfish has evolved the capacity to cover its body with the same chemical. The tentacles think the fish is one of them and so it lives a charmed life, protected from other predators.' He thinks, too, that the clownfish does the anemone a service by luring other fish into range of its lethal tentacles and serving as a 'cleaner upper' of irritating waste matter by eating left-overs.

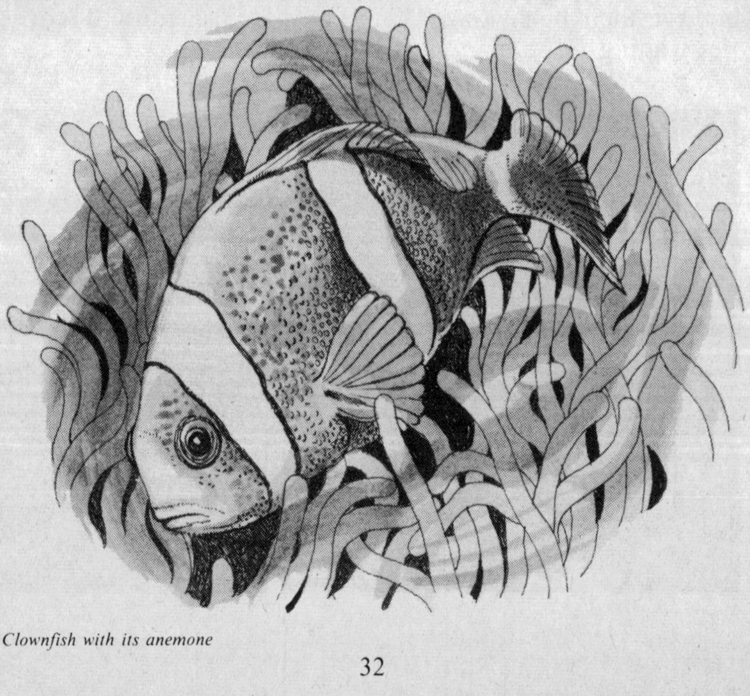

Clownfish with its anemone

As an example of how continual fish-watching can lead to new theories Peter Scott compares what he saw on two separate dives ten years apart. In 1956 he got to know one particular clownfish and anemone in Fiji. When he dived on the same reef ten years later, an anemone was still in exactly the same place with its family of clownfish. He thinks it is possible that groups of clownfish make the same anemone their home for years on end.

In the waters of the Red Sea there is a myriad of other strange and beautiful marine life. Pufferfish cruise near the wreck of the *Umbria*. The puffer can do exactly what its name implies. When it's threatened or frightened it puffs itself up with air or water to look rather like a small football or balloon, probably to make it appear, to a predator, too large to be eaten.

Many of the fish of the coral reefs are brightly coloured and patterned and this has a function in nature. It can be a warning to predators that you are poisonous or taste nasty or it can be a threat display, very off-putting to someone

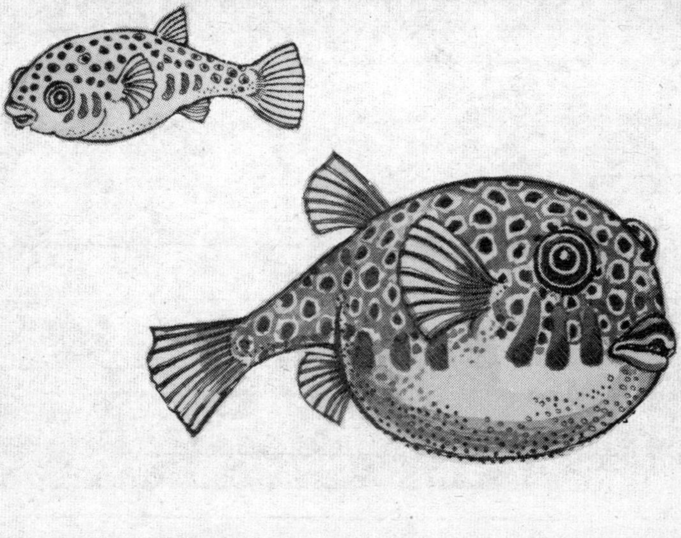

Pufferfish normal size and puffed up

you are about to attack. Peter Scott found this out about a male of a fish species called Anthius simply by watching it. He saw the fish change its head colour from purplish to bright blue as it prepared to attack a rival.

The surgeon fish, however, has something more effective. It carries a pair of sharp knives each side of its body in front of the tail fin. These knives are normally depressed as if in sheaths. In attack or defence, out they come and the fish lashes its tail to use them to the best advantage.

Deeper down, in the very bottom-most hold of the *Umbria, Survival* divers found nocturnal squirrel fish with huge eyes that help them to search for food in the dark.

The crannies of the wreck held moray eels, which have to be treated with some respect. A moray eel keeps its powerful body, which can be up to two metres in length, out of sight and just exposes its head and its needle-sharp teeth. It can move with lightning speed and sometimes attacks divers, inflicting serious, tearing wounds.

Moray eel

5
WHERE HIM OF THE HAIRY HANDS LIVES

Off the coast of Andros Island, one of the Bahamas group near the Gulf of Mexico, is a sea of mystery. The local fishermen will tell you a monster called the 'Lusca' lives here, a giant, squid-like creature that not only devours human beings but can drag a whole ship and her crew into the depths. The monster, they say, lives in the mysterious 'Blue Holes' so called because the deep water in them makes them show up blue against the white of the coral shelf.

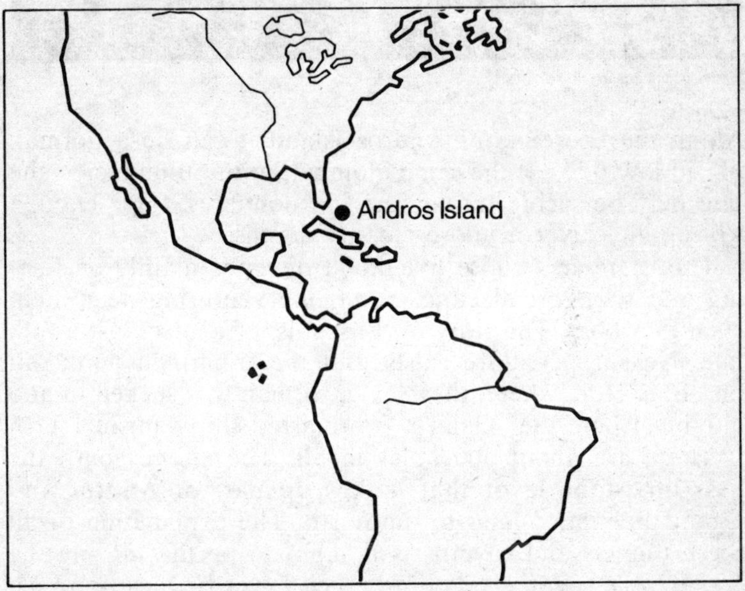

The Blue Holes are deep caves, some in the sea, some inland on Andros Island itself. The seaward holes teem with fish, such as sardines, pilchards, anchovies, grunts and snappers, and these bring, in their wake, those voracious hunters of the sea, the sharks. The tidal currents that race through many of the holes are fierce and unpredictable.

Shoal of anchovies

Along the shoreline of Andros Island it can be a normal, placid low tide. At the same moment, in the Blue Holes, the tide may be racing through at 15 kilometres, force enough to trap any diver in those gloomy depths.

The islanders, whose livelihood depends mainly on fishing and sponge collecting, don't like venturing near them even in a boat. The story of 'Lusca' is, of course, just a folk tale. No such creature exists. But the fishermen point out one Blue Hole where, they say, a woman was sucked in and another where they claim a two-masted ship vanished.

There are about 300 holes in all. They honeycomb the vast limestone layer that makes up part of Andros and Grand Bahama Island to the north. The explanation of all these tunnels and caverns is thought to be that during the Ice Age the ocean levels were much lower because so much water had turned to ice. Much of the limestone around the Bahamas was then above sea level. Over many millions of years, rains gnawed tunnels in this exposed porous rock. Then, as the world emerged from the Ice Age and the great thaw came, the level of the ocean rose again and the sea flooded the tunnels.

This is about all that was known about the Blue Holes when Don and Kathy Renn went to Andros Island for *Survival* to make a film about them. And there were questions to which they wanted answers. Did most of the holes connect? Were some of the holes, many kilometres inland, connected with those out at sea?

Kathy set off inland with a local guide and found a lagoon three kilometres from the sea, set among thick mangroves. Andros is 64 kilometres across and much of it is covered with freshwater swamps — but this lagoon was salt water. In it were the kinds of fish found on coral reefs: surgeon fish, grunts and snappers. The fish must have got there from the sea. It seemed obvious that the holes did connect, probably through a chain of tunnels too narrow for a man to pass through, but Don decided to experiment.

He placed some barracuda heads as shark bait in a Blue Hole in the sea and some more in a nearby inland hole. The sharks went for the bait in the seaward hole and then appeared in the inland hole, attracted by the bait there, too. Once again, proof of a connection. The sharks concerned were lemon sharks, well known for their ferocity and

Surgeon fish side view, and head on showing one of its two knives just in front of tail

aggressiveness when attacking large prey fish like tuna. Don found half a dozen stranded in the inland hole, at least until the tide changed or until they chose to swim back to the sea down the narrow tunnel. It was a unique opportunity to film them in, more or less, captive conditions. So Don got into the water with them with only his underwater camera between himself and their voracious jaws.

For the next stage of their filmed investigation the Renns decided to go deep — to plumb one of the most formidable holes, well over 80 metres deep. Kathy went down with a powerful light, feeling the water getting rapidly colder and darker. At 60 metres visibility was down to a few centimetres. If ever there was a place for the fabulous 'Lusca' to dwell this was it. But all Kathy met were snappers, grunts and some angel fish. But at the very bottom she discovered positive proof that these limestone caverns had once been above the level of the sea. She found stalactites and stalagmites encrusted with coral and algae that could have been formed only by the action of dripping water millions of years ago.

It will need many dives over many years to build up a complete picture of the ramifications of the Blue Holes, but Don and Kathy were the first to film some of their secrets.

Kathy Renn entering Blue Hole off Andros Island

6
THE WORLD OF THE BEAVER

A pond high in the Rocky Mountains of Wyoming wouldn't exist at all if a family of small animals hadn't built a dam across a swiftly flowing mountain river.

The expression 'working like a beaver' isn't an empty one. The beaver is just about the busiest little creature imaginable. Although beavers work to create conditions favourable to themselves, much of it is also beneficial to man. They are great drainage engineers and by damming mountain streams help to conserve water where it is most needed.

Beavers have many other admirable qualities. When they mate they remain loyal to each other for the rest of their lives. Should one die the other will not mate again. They are excellent, though stern, parents. When a young beaver reaches the mature age of two years it is driven out by its parents in the early spring because the room and food reserve will be needed for the new members of the family, called kits, that will be born in May. If the two-year-olds won't go, the parents may even kill them.

When a two-year-old leaves home it looks for a mate. Together they search for a stream to dam so that they can create their own pond and build their own home, called a lodge. They build a dam for several good beaver reasons. They like a moat round their home so that it is harder for their natural enemies, like the bear, to get at them. And by flooding a large area behind the dam they make it easy to tow back branches of trees they cut down to build their lodge.

To make the dam they pile stones on the stream bed and build upwards by wedging in twigs and branches and using layers of mud. The building of the lodge is a skilful job. Some people think that beavers make their lodge hollow like an igloo. What they really do is pile up sticks and branches and then hollow out their living chamber by

Beaver preparing to fell a birch tree

Beaver with kits

working underwater. They use a mud cement to hold the whole thing together, dredging up load after load and carrying it between chin and forepaws. The pile of branches may look a bit slapdash but, in fact, they are all cunningly interwoven.

In between all this hard work of felling trees with their long, chisel-like teeth, the beavers are stuffing themselves with leaves and young shoots. By early autumn, however, a fresh duty awaits them. They must prepare for the coming winter by cutting off leafy branches, which they tow into the pond and stick in the mud at the bottom close to their lodge, so that — no matter how severe the ice and snow of the winter to come — they have those branches underwater for food. The leaves will die but the bark will still be good to eat.

The beaver has another clever survival trick. It dredges deep-water channels where normal winter ice will never reach. Thus there is always an ice-free underwater corridor between the larder of branches and the lodge. This forward planning on the part of the beaver is quite extraordinary.

Instinctively the animal knows that all its hard work in laying up that winter stock of food would be wasted if it were trapped in the lodge by ice all around it. And there is one duty a beaver never forgets — the regular inspection of a dam to make sure there is no leakage of water that could begin as a trickle and gradually tear a big hole in the construction.

A beaver is well equipped by nature for its underwater life. When diving, the ears and nose are closed by valves and transparent eyelids act like skin diver's goggles. The heart beat slows down so less oxygen is used up.

Most beavers do their eating and tree-felling at night (centuries of persecution by hunters and trappers have made them largely nocturnal). But they are not always too intelligent about tree-felling. They give themselves a lot of extra work because, often, a tree they have cut down gets caught

Inside a beaver's lodge

A skunk visits the dam

up in the branches of another one nearby. The beaver never seems to think of cutting the second one down too, so that it could have two trees for the price of one! It just writes off the first one and goes away to another tree.

This over-enthusiasm for work is evident in dam-building too. Often beavers will build a dam, say, 200 metres long when a short distance upstream, if they had been able to work it out, they could have dammed the river with only a fifty-metre-wide wall. Yet they know by instinct how to curve a dam to resist the pressure of water.

The most fascinating thing about the beaver's engineering is the help it provides, unwittingly, for many other creatures. Everything seems to take advantage of the beaver's pond. Moose enjoy willow shoots that have sprouted because beavers felled the trees and let the sunlight in. The pond draws wildfowl, racoons, opossums, porcupine, even the non-poisonous garter snake, an excellent swimmer, who is no menace to the beavers, but grabs and swallows any unwary frog or toad that may be around.

Beavers are not only marvellous drainage and construction engineers — mankind owes them a great deal because they stop erosion by damming. A lot of mountain meadows, now fertile, are on the sites of old beaver dams. Beavers occasionally kill valuable trees and sometimes their engineering results in flooded roads and railway cuttings.

But there is one clumsy and destructive invader for whom the beaver has a wary respect — the grizzly bear. Not that the bear can do much about catching a beaver in its lodge. The beaver is smart enough to build bolt holes round the banks of its pond into which it can swim in moments of danger. It is only when a beaver is cornered on land that it is in trouble, because the bear is bigger and moves faster. Failing to trap the beaver on land, the bear will have a go at trying to wreck the beaver's lodge, but he's not often successful. The beaver builds too well and deep.

Today, besides North America, the beaver survives in Europe, mainly in Norway, Sweden, Germany, Poland and Russia, where it is strictly protected. In Britain it is believed to have become extinct in about the twelfth century. Man was responsible. It was killed for its fur and meat and for a glandular secretion that was quite falsely believed to have curative powers.

7
THE TROUT AND THE MAYFLY

It's late May and the countryside is in full bloom. The fly fisherman is busy casting his artificial dry-fly on the clear waters of a trout stream. If he is skilful and delicate in his casting his fly may be mistaken by a trout for the real thing — a large, handsome insect called a mayfly which hatches out at this time of the year. For the biggest trout, who may never bother with flies the rest of the year, the mayfly is such a delicacy that it will risk coming to the surface from the weedy depths to snatch greedily at it, losing a lot of its usual caution.

Survival asked a remarkable group called Oxford Scientific Films to study and record the underwater lives of both the trout and its victim, the mayfly. This task included filming the spawning process of the trout and the complicated stages the mayfly goes through before it emerges as a creature of shimmering wings; also many other secrets of nature hidden beneath the surface of a trout stream.

But how could all this intricate interplay of life among creatures underwater at different times of the year be studied and recorded on film? Oxford Scientific's answer was to build their own river in the studio so that their cameras could be placed in an ideal position for close-up filming which would have been impossible in a real trout stream.

First, they constructed a tank that was five metres long and held 4,500 litres of water. But much, much more had to be done. You don't fill a tank with water, put some trout in and expect them to live naturally. The scientists had to apply what they knew of the trout's life and spawning to the building of the stream. The water in a trout stream is fast flowing, so they used a pump to reproduce the powerful flow of a chalk stream. The water had to be the right temperature. Trout spawn during the coldest months of winter in water that is down to 4° or 5° Centigrade, so they installed a milk-cooling machine to achieve this.

Next, the exact conditions of a natural spawning bed had to be created. To hatch out successfully, trout eggs need a constant flow of water along the bed of the river and among the pebbles of the gravel in which they are buried. Boulders were designed and positioned so that they would cause bottom eddies that would drive the water right down into the gravel. Rotating propellors created the wind ripples over the surface of the water and, finally, the two nicest touches of all were added — a device for back projection to give a background of growing plants and weed beds, and a gadget that released debris, such as small pieces of weed and twigs, to float with the current.

By the time the Oxford scientists were finished any self-respecting trout would have accepted that tank as a pleasant stretch of river in the English countryside. Certainly, the brown trout they obtained from a hatchery settled down nicely in this man-made river.

John Paling filming the 'trout stream'

From November through to January the female trout lays eggs on gravelly shallows called a redd. The female has a lot of work to do preparing the nest in the gravel. By rapid movements of the tail that whip up a current, she cuts a hole in the river bed gravel in which the eggs are to be laid. At this time the males queue up just down stream, fighting among themselves for a female's favour.

It was a magical moment when spawning actually occurred. Joined by a male, the female began shedding the eggs, which the male fertilised with milt. In running water, milt and eggs have just two seconds to make contact. The cup-shaped nest made by the female in the river bed helps to keep sperm and eggs together for those vital seconds. Almost immediately the female begins to cover the fertilised eggs with gravel, lifting quite large stones by powerful and rapid beats of the tail. As when digging out the nest, she doesn't actually touch the gravel with her tail but whips up a current, which does the job.

The trout eggs lie buried in the gravel for three cold

Female trout laying eggs in artificial stream

winter months. After about one hundred days, the life within them begins to emerge. The very small fry are called alevins. Nature thoughtfully provides them with a bulging yolk sac of nourishment beneath the throat so that, defenceless as they are, they don't expose themselves to danger in hunting food.

At the end of three weeks they begin to look like little fish called fingerlings. By the end of a month they have developed into miniature trout. From the moment the eggs are laid casualties are very high. But nature provides for this too. A female trout lays seven or eight thousand eggs. Only a tiny percentage become adult fish. Indeed, when you come to think of it, only one pair need to survive to spawn themselves, to keep the population steady.

No stream is a paradise to trout, and the Oxford scientists filmed three creatures that feed on both trout eggs and trout — the pike, the chub and a remarkable bird called the dipper.

The pike — sometimes called the freshwater shark — will eat almost any fish but shows a marked preference for trout.

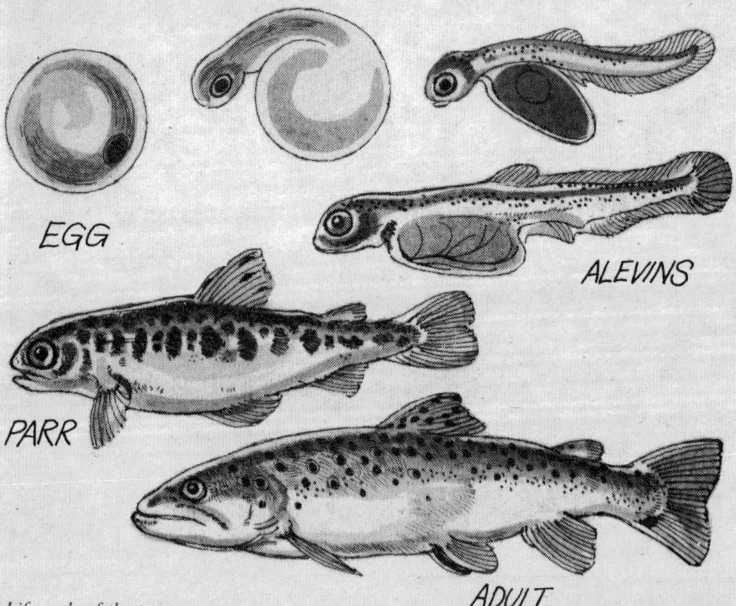

Life cycle of the trout

Dipper 'flying' under water while searching for food

Chub will gobble any small fish. But it is the dipper, a small brown and white bird that can 'fly' and walk underwater to feed on trout eggs, who is the star predator.

The scientists obtained a permit to catch a dipper in the Forest of Dean and were delighted when the bird settled down happily in their artificial river. They were ready to release it if it had not. Dippers live mainly on stony mountain streams and, occasionally, on south country chalk rivers. As it 'flies' underwater using its wings as it would in the air, bubbles trapped in its feathers make it look like a silver dart. Sometimes it clings to or moves quite large stones searching for trout eggs. During its four-week stay in the tank it ate one thousand trout eggs as well as thousands of freshwater shrimps specially provided for it.

The mayfly's life is quite as fraught with danger as is the trout's. For up to three years the larvae of this beautiful insect live in the bottom silt, sometimes swimming about freely and always at the risk of their lives, not only from hungry fish but from other fiercely predatory insects, such as the larvae of the dragonfly.

A newly hatched mayfly

Over the years of its underwater life it splits its skin time and time again in order to grow larger. Each split heralds a new stage of growth, which the scientist calls an 'instar'.

Then, at last, comes the miraculous day of emergence. Why miraculous? Because on every river that has a hatch of mayfly, the larvae — fishermen call them 'nymphs' — rise to the surface during the same fortnight of the year, either in late May or early June, according to the river. The larva swims upwards and splits its skin at the surface. There emerges a large and lovely fly with three tails, a yellow, segmented body and four upright transparent wings. The trout fishermen know this mayfly as a 'dun', dun because its wings are still dun-coloured and covered with a dull, transparent skin. This skin has yet to be shed.

The fascinating thing about the dun which was filmed in close-up emerging from its case, or 'shuck', was that it has no mouth or stomach. It exists for one day only — simply to find a mate and breed. The duns flutter away from the surface of the stream, but many are eaten by trout even as they hatch. While those that escape are making that first

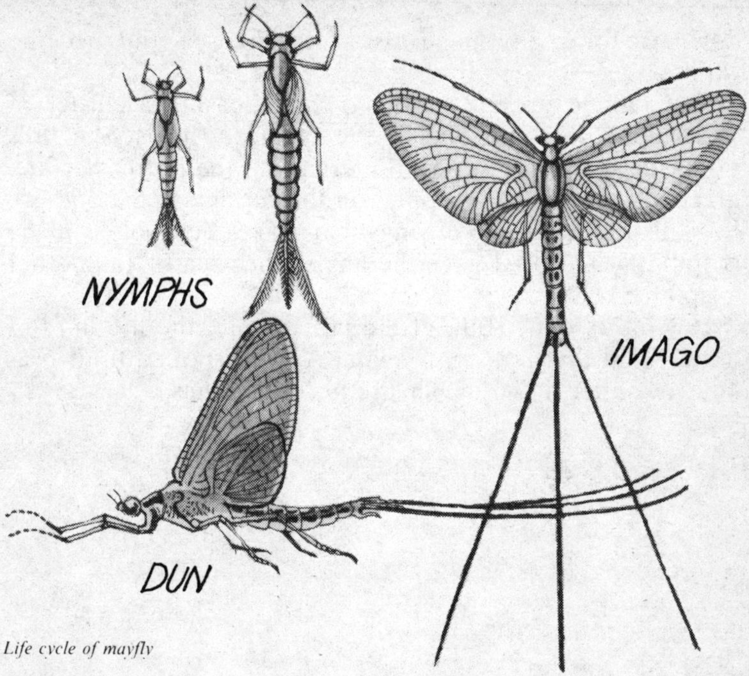

Life cycle of mayfly

flight, all kinds of birds — swallows, swifts, martins and even sparrows — catch them in mid-air. The survivors shelter in the bankside vegetation and there they perform the last fantastic transformation. They split their final skin and emerge as the shining, perfect insect whose body and wings shimmer as if coated with fine varnish. The scientist calls them at this stage *imagos* — the angler knows them as 'spinners'.

Now the last act of their drama is about to begin. That evening, twenty-four hours after they first hatched, the males perform a rising and falling wedding flight in the shelter of a bush or tree. A female flies into this swarm, is seized in mid-air and fertilised. Once the female has been fertilized, the male dies. The female immediately flies back to the river to lay her eggs before she dies. The female mayfly flies *upstream* to drop her eggs in order to make up for the distance lost by the larvae, the previous day, when they drifted downstream in the current to hatch. If the female spinner didn't make this upstream allowance, all the mayfly in the world would long ago have ended up further downstream until they finished in the sea and became extinct.

The female presses on upstream, releasing a cluster of eggs each time she touches the surface. At last she falls exhausted on to the water, fluttering out the last of her life, making a circle of tiny ripples on the surface as she does so. It is this pulsing circle of rings that makes her look as if she is spinning and first gave the angler the idea of calling her a 'spinner'.

Her job is done. But, at the last minute, the life lines of mayfly and the trout cross again. A great spotted trout rises and sucks her down as her useful life finishes.

8
THE WORLD YOU NEVER SEE

Have you ever stopped to think how much the human eye *cannot* see? How little we know of life going on all around us because of the limited power and range of our vision? Scientists, of course, can study minute subjects with such aids as the enormously powerful electron microscope, but now new camera techniques are bringing this world-you-never-see to the television screens for all of us to share.

For instance, 'time-lapse' photography can show us through the eye of the camera the whole process of a flower opening its petals to the sun, or a moth emerging from a chrysalis. By exposing one frame of film every half hour, say, instead of the normal twenty-four frames a second, it is possible to compress in a few seconds a happening that takes many hours in nature.

Dr John Paling, freshwater biologist with Oxford Scientific Films, filmed an extraordinary sequence showing how puffballs, a kind of fungus that grows on rotten tree trunks, distribute their spores. The mechanism is like this: each puffball is filled with a cloud of spores and has a hole in its domed top through which these spores can escape. But they need some force to drive them out. In early winter, when the leaves are stripped from the trees, the puffball waits ready and primed like a miniature minefield. In fact, all it needs is a rainy day to provide the detonator. Then, after rain, on the bare branches above it, the detonator hangs poised — a super-drop of collected rain water. A normal raindrop is not heavy enough to punch out the spores in the puffball but, as the trees dry out after rain, heavy drops continue to collect and fall on the puffball, punching it as a fist strikes a punchball and sending out a burst of spores with each punch.

Gerald Thompson, entomologist of the group, uses what is called cold light to film insects. The heat generated by

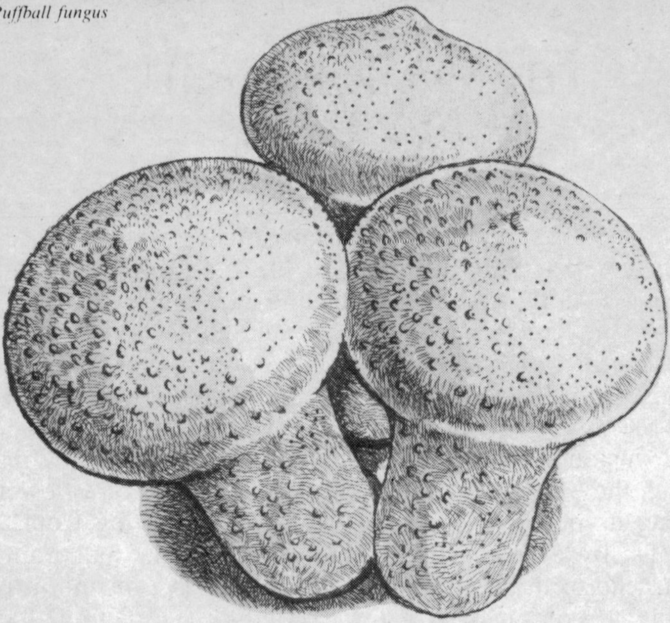

Puffball fungus

normal powerful film lights would kill insects in seconds, so with the clever use of filters and lamps enclosed in flasks of water, he takes the heat out of the lights. In this way with a high-powered lens, he was able to film a mosquito — a creature of the air — emerging from the pupa that lives in water. The legs are coiled inside the pupa like a spring. Thompson's cameras showed in slow motion how they unwind. The head of the pupa cracks open ready for the mosquito to exchange life in the water for life in the air. In the world of the high-powered lens, water isn't water as we see it. It seems to be covered with a layer of colourless plastic — the surface film as it is called. Once a mosquito is free, it slides across this film at every breath of the wind, as if it were skating on ice.

Man is now busy drilling in the North Sea for oil. Millions of pounds' worth of cumbersome machinery is being used for this job. Some insects can carry their own powerful drilling machinery as Gerald Thompson demonstrated. Would you imagine that an insect can drill deep into a living pine tree? The wood wasp, an insect over two centi-

Life cycle of the mosquito

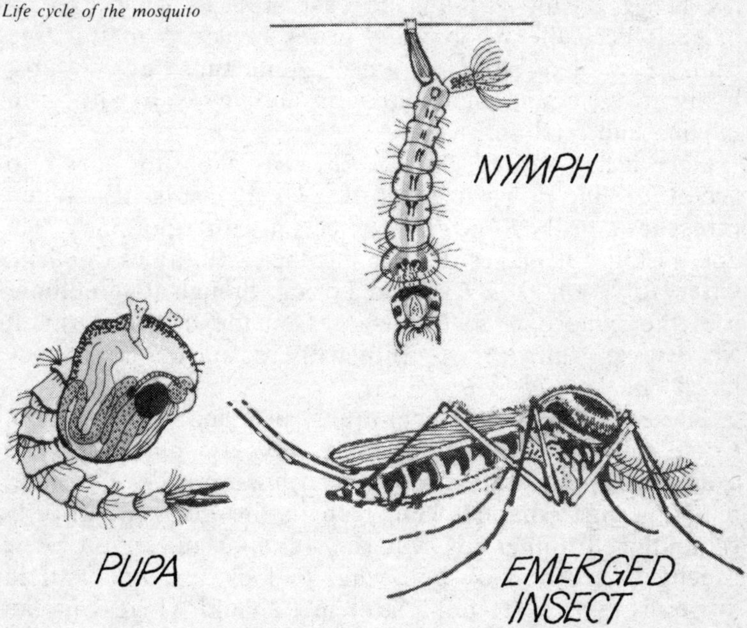

metres long, prospects conifer trees for a suitable spot to lay its eggs. When it finds one, it brings into use its ovipositor (egg-laying organ), a thin blade that it uses like a high-powered drill. And what a beautiful piece of engineering this blade is. It has three sections, called stylets, which slide one against the other. Carried behind the insect's body is a sheath to house the blade when it is not in use. The wasp drills a hole more than two centimetres deep into the wood and ejects the eggs from a hole at the drill's tip. With the eggs all cosy and hidden and with plenty of wood for the grubs to eat, the wood wasp pulls its ovipositor out of the tree and goes happily on its way. If the grubs are left alone to chew enough wood to grow large and fat, they will emerge in two years' time as the next generation of wood wasps.

But the wood wasp might not be quite so happy if he knew what often happens as soon as his back is turned. Enter the ichneumon fly, the villain of the piece, *Rhyssa persuasoria.* This fly intends to lay its eggs too — but not for its young to feed on wood. It has a very different idea — to lay its eggs on top of the wood wasp grub. But first it has to detect where the wood wasp grubs lie, deep in the tree trunk. How it does this no one is quite sure but it is probably by detecting the faint vibration made by the grub moving and feeding.

Once it has located a grub, *Rhyssa*'s ovipositor goes into action, drilling down to reach the wood wasp grubs. When it reaches a grub, *Rhyssa* first injects it with a poison, which doesn't kill but makes it dormant, then withdraws the drill. Often *Rhyssa* makes a second boring, though it sometimes uses the same one, to lay its eggs on top of the dormant wood wasp grub. *Rhyssa* grubs will feed on this when they hatch out.

These new camera techniques also enabled Dr John Cook, one of the world's leading experts on spiders, to examine a species called *Atypus. Atypus,* a purse-web spider, makes a cigar-shaped web deep in the grass, a skilfully camouflaged tunnel you would never spot unless you knew exactly where to look and what to look for. Box Hill in Surrey is one of the few places in England where you can find *Atypus.*

A giant wood wasp with 'drill' in position

Atypus, a purse-web spider

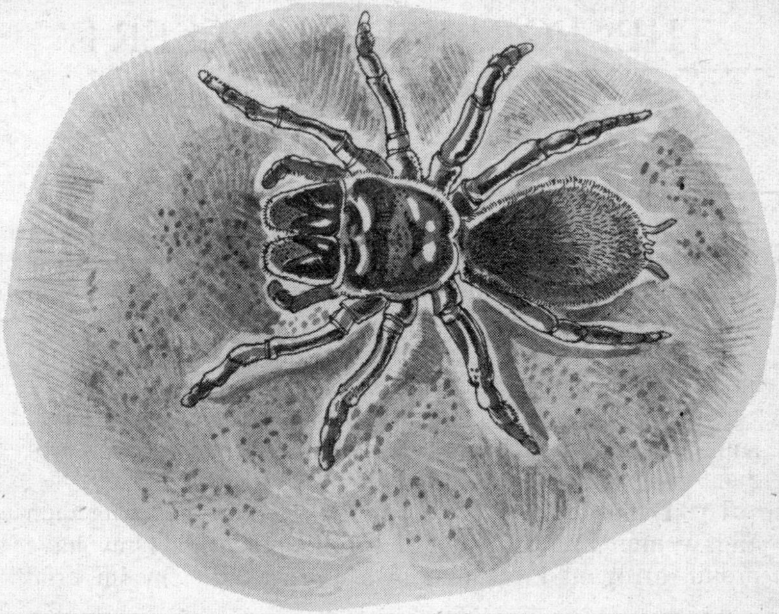

Inside the cocoon-like web *Atypus* waits. When an insect lands on the web, the vibration tells the spider that something is at the larder door. Inside its tunnel it moves to a position exactly beneath the unsuspecting fly and suddenly lunges its fangs upwards through the web, grabbing it and injecting poison. When the fly stops struggling, the spider cuts a hole in its own web and drags the victim down. Having got its next meal safely stashed away, it repairs the tell-tale hole in the roof ready for the next victim to arrive.

Another spider, *Segestria,* lives in old brickwork. It is an angler among spiders — in fact, it is often known as the fishing-line spider. It spins fine lines outwards over the brickwork from the hole where it has its lair. There it sits, feeling the lines, like some alert angler waiting for a bite. When a fly or bee touches one of the lines the 'bite' is detected by one of *Segestria*'s feet. But the spider doesn't haul in anything. The hook on these lines is *Segestria* itself. It darts out and seizes the victim and carries it back to its parlour to eat.

9
THE FORBIDDEN DESERT OF THE DANAKIL

The Danakil desert of Ethiopia, at the southern end of the Red Sea, has a landscape that looks like a giant's slag heap. Huge grey lava flows claw out across the desert. In places the earth is stained yellow with sulphur and red from iron deposits thrown up by volcanic action. Whole hillsides smoke as if made of fire and brimstone. There are several active volcanoes and many dormant ones.

It seems impossible that anyone can live in such a harsh land — but it does produce a case-hardened human product, the Danakil tribesmen.

The Danakil are a handsome people whose young men and women are slim and naturally graceful. They have proud, arrogant faces that owe more to ancient Imperial

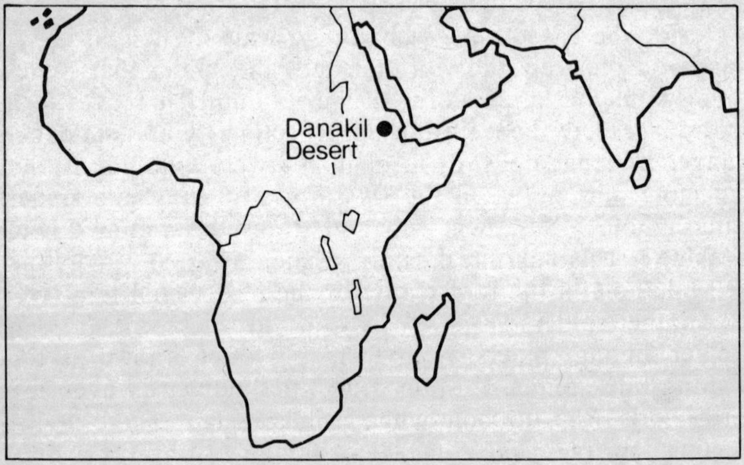

Egypt than to the African bush. They are of the Moslem faith. They have the reputation of being one of the most hostile peoples in the world.

A cameraman would be in serious danger trying to film these people unless he had safe conduct from the Sultan of

Aussa, His Excellency Bitwoded Ali Mirah Hanfare, the absolute ruler of the Danakil. The Sultan lives in a modest palace in his capital, Asaita, and it was there that Colin Willock, head of the *Survival* team, and cameraman Dieter Plage asked for permission and protection in the making of a film.

Both Colin and Dieter are unlikely to forget their first encounter with the Danakil warriors. 'They look at you as a hawk looks at you, with a cold, contemptuous, appraising eye. Meet them in the desert and there they are, tall and straight, standing motionless, sometimes leaning on a rifle, but more often, carrying it across their shoulders with wrists looped at either end over the muzzle and stock. You have a very distinct feeling that it would take very little to have them looking down the rifle sights at you. . . .

However, their interview went well. When they were ushered into the audience room of the palace they found the imposing figure of the Sultan seated at a plain table on which stood an alarm clock. They had been told that when the alarm clock sounded, the interview would be at an end. Their talk was eased by hospitable cups of coffee flavoured with pepper and camel's milk. At the end of the interview, the Sultan gave both his permission and his assurance of a personal bodyguard for Dieter when he began filming. The Sultan was well aware that the coming of modern civilisation would change the way of life of the Danakil and that a film story of his people before that change overtook them would be a valuable historical record.

The Danakil have a history of murder and mutilation and in their barren desert land old customs still partially survive. All the warriors, even today, carry a 40 centimetre-long knife, curved and razor sharp on both edges. This fearsome-looking knife, carried horizontally at the waist, is as natural a part of their everyday dress as a watch or a pen is to a European. Of course, the Sultan actively discourages the practice of the Danakil raiding their neighbours for trophies, but they still go on in secret, sometimes against a tribe called the Issa, a section of Somalis. Dieter filmed a Danakil warrior wearing a black ostrich feather in his hair, a certain sign that he had recently killed his first victim, thus

proving, in the eyes of other warriors, his manhood.

The burning desert where the temperatures can rise to 55 degrees Centigrade and more, has a profound effect on the character of the people, but there is more to it than that. The chief reason why, down the ages, the Danakil have murdered foreigners who have visited their territory is water — or rather the lack of it.

They have just one river, called the Awash. It plunges down 3,000 metres from the Ethiopian Highlands and by the time it reaches the Danakil desert it is large and powerful. But it never reaches the Red Sea. Like some tired animal, it halts 130 kilometres from the sea, breaks up into channels and finally ends up as a vast, shimmering lake called Abbé, where its waters are sucked up into the sky by evaporation as fast as the Awash delivers.

Water has the value of gold in the desert. Danakil warriors will murder to protect a muddy water hole because it might well have to serve one whole tribal area and its animals, so you can imagine what the Awash river means to them. The Awash with the narrow band of fertility along its

Danakil warriors armed with rifle and long knives

banks is so precious that they will kill any foreigner who goes near it. To them it is protecting a strip of paradise in a hell hole. In fact they protected it so well that it wasn't until 1934 that the mystery of the disappearing Awash was solved.

The man who solved it, and risked his life to do so, was a British explorer named Wilfred Thesiger. He was twenty-three when he set out from Addis Ababa into a country where he knew that at least three expeditions had attempted to trace the course of the Awash and had all vanished never to be seen again. Yet young as Thesiger was, he knew Ethiopia well. He was born in 1910 in one of the mud huts that housed the British Legation in Addis Ababa, where his father was British Minister. He was educated in Britain, returned to Ethiopia when he was twenty and it was from another British explorer, Colonel Cheesman, that he first heard about the mystery of the Awash.

Thesiger saw country that had never been seen by a white man before — or, at least, a white man who remained alive to tell the story. In one village he visited, the headman had just died and was to be succeeded by his son. However, the son was not regarded as a warrior since he had killed only one man. But on the day Wilfred Thesiger arrived the son returned from a raid on the Issi during which he had shot three men dead.

The aftermath of this raid is described in Thesiger's words. 'There was a tremendous feast and celebration going on. I stayed there a few days and the day after I had left I heard that raiders from the other side of the Awash river had wiped out the village, killing the young new headman and every single person in it. The raiders were another section of the Danakil tribe.'

The Danakil are nomadic, that is, they simply move on to some other spot when their stock have eaten all the grazing. Building a home for a week or a month is nearly as easy for them as pitching a tent. The roof over their heads is made up of mats that are thrown over a framework of bent sticks.

The basic unit of a Danakil group is a homestead. It consists of one wife and a family hut. The wife and mother is a greatly respected figure, although the senior male heads the hamlet or group of homesteads. The wife is expected to supervise all the domestic chores, such as making ghee, the goat-milk butter that serves as nutriment as well as a dressing for the hair. It's the young, unmarried girls who do most of the housework. When they become of a marriageable age, around seventeen, they are usually betrothed to a cousin or a distant member of the clan. This is designed to ensure family unity. The husband will expect his young wife to be efficient in such domestic jobs as pounding maize in a wooden mortar; if he is a relative, he will pay only a token bride price, perhaps one cow or one sheep or an equivalent three goats.

The young warriors consider themselves as an elite and they do little or no work. Milk, warm from the camel, is their staple diet. They seldom touch meat except at a feast, perhaps after a battle.

In their day-to-day lives, several families often band together to herd their goats as a measure of defence against raiders. Frequently, children who share the herding remain close friends for life, even if they are simply neighbours and not related.

Danakil women and child

Dieter filmed a market day in Asaita. For the tribesmen and their families it was a matter of trading a surplus of anything they had for anything they needed. Goat-milk butter in exchange for a mat or a skin (goat skin is a prime commodity as a water container). Most of the goods bartered are scanty local produce but there are a few town goods, such as fabrics and plastic sandals brought in from the Ethiopian Highlands by traders at some personal risk. As an example of the gentler side of the Danakil nature, Dieter noticed that kinsfolk kiss each other's hands as a greeting when they meet.

When Dieter was filming the Danakil he had to be very careful. He hid his camera in the window of a house nearby because he knew that the tribesmen hated cameras and, in particular, they hated their women being filmed. If he had openly turned his camera on the women, the men would almost certainly have turned violent. Dieter had learned this lesson earlier when he had shown his camera to a group of warriors and invited them to see their friends through the little black box. He thought it would amuse them. It had the opposite effect. They turned very nasty and threatening, and later Dieter was told by his interpreter that he had been very close to being attacked.

Market day in Asaita. The camels await the return of their owners

10
THE EMPTY DESERT

Four thousand kilometres away from the Danakil, right across the African continent to the south-west, there is another wild place where it would be impossible for man to settle, but where there are living creatures that somehow wring an existence from it. It is the oldest desert in the world, the Namib, a sea of red sand 800 kilometres wide stretching down the coast of South West Africa from Angola to the South African border. Rain in the Namib is as rare as a London street paved with gold. It is intensely hot and the burning, shifting sand piles up gigantic dunes more than 300 metres high. It was in this pitiless desert that husband and wife team Rod and Moira Borland spent six months filming for *Survival.*

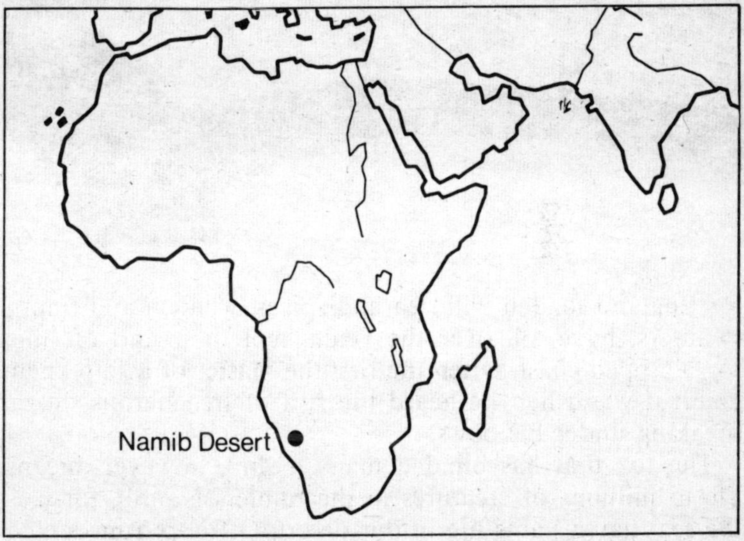

The Namib is bordered by a seashore with the sinister name of the Skeleton Coast, a graveyard of hundreds of ships and their crews. Great waves lash this coast, having travelled 3,200 kilometres across the Atlantic ocean. Windjammers rounding the Cape of Good Hope on course

Dried up 'vlei' or flood pan in the Namib desert

for England loaded with tea and spices, whalers and tramp steamers, have all, over the years, met their end off this fog-wrapped coast. Often the first the master of a ship knew about it was when he heard the surf of treacherous shoals breaking under his bows.

The fog that has blinded many a ship, however, means life to millions of creatures in the rainless Namib, for it is the sea that sustains life in this desert. Offshore runs a cold Antarctic current called the Benguella. When the heated air of the desert merges with the colder atmosphere of the Benguella, a morning belt of fog is produced. This fog condenses into life-giving droplets of water on the surface of the sand, on rocks and on the leaves of the sparse vegeta-

Giant dunes and dead trees killed by seasonal floods in the Namib desert

tion. If this didn't happen every living creature in the Namib would soon die.

Small animals and insects have adapted to these severe conditions in extraordinary ways. Each species had its own way of getting its meagre supply of water from the blessing of the fog. There's the beetle, locally called a Tok-Tokky, which has a built-in water-saving system. It has wing cases on which the fog condenses. It carries a sort of roof gutter round the outside of the wing cases to catch this water. It has long hind legs so that it can tilt itself forward to bring the water to a slot that delivers the water into its mouth.

How do the insects and animals find food? Nature obliges grudgingly. Seeds and grasses, driven hundreds of kilo-

The gerbil eats grass seeds, deriving from them sufficient moisture to survive in the rainless Namib desert

The rare golden mole, an eyeless creature, that burrows through the sand in search of insects

Trapdoor spider digging its hole in the sand

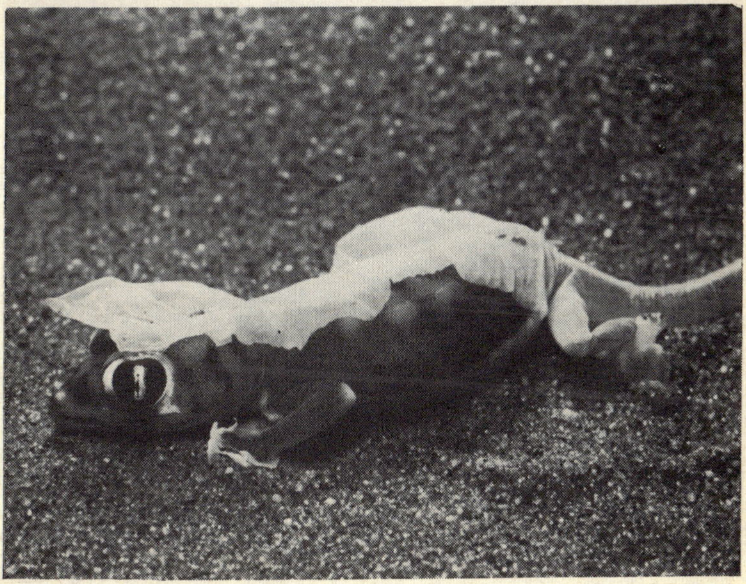

Palmatto gekko shedding its old skin

metres by the wind, collect in little hollows of the giant sand dunes and the small animals know they can find food there.

But how do they manage to live in the intense heat when the surface temperature of the desert can top 55 degrees Centigrade? Those water-saving beetles use their long legs to keep their bodies away from the sizzling surface. A beetle-hunting lizard with the impressive name of *Aporosaurus* spends the day making quick sorties to the hot side of a sand dune, where it collects food and then dashes back to the cooler side until it is ready for another mad dash for a meal. This lizard has an ingenious method of avoiding the boiling-hot sand for any length of time: it raises its tail, then its body and eventually alternate feet from the surface.

Then there is the golden mole whose coat has a lovely metallic sheen. It burrows in the sand, but unlike the common mole we know in Britain it doesn't throw up mounds. Another lizard hunts only at night and, like the mole, lies buried in the sand in the day, away from the burning rays of the sun. The trapdoor spider makes not only a hole in the sand but fixes a manhole or trapdoor by binding grains of sand with a web. Another desert spider, the white lady, performs a strange ritual dance that, as yet, has not been scientifically explained.

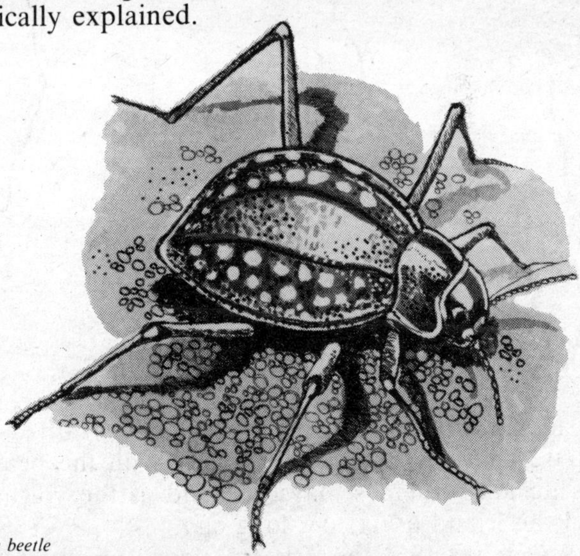

Tok-Tokky beetle

11
THE LONELIEST PLACE IN THE WORLD

Move out into the bleak loneliness of the middle of the Atlantic ocean and you come to a place exposed like a raw thumb to the fury of gales and big seas and, on one famous occasion, to the threat of an erupting volcano. Tristan da Cunha is such an isolated little island it is sometimes called the loneliest place in the world. In fact, it is one of a group of three volcanic islands, but it is the only one inhabited by man. The other two islands, Nightingale and Inaccessible, are inhabited by sea birds. The Tristans, as the islanders are called, had every reason to be thankful in 1961 that those islands were there when a volcano on their own island erupted.

Tristan has one settlement of about two hundred people.

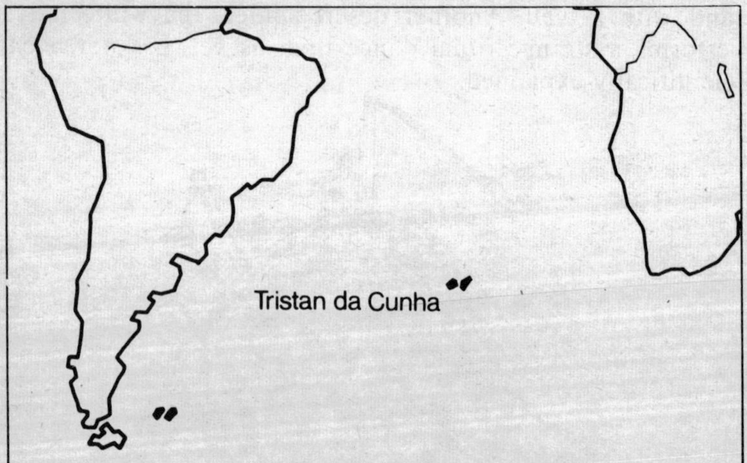

Their houses crouch on a narrow plain beneath towering, 600-metre-high cliff walls. Still higher, with the peak 2,100 metres up and lost most days in cloud, is the volcano that created the island of Tristan long ago.

On 9 October 1961 the Tristans awoke to ominous rumblings. But it wasn't the big volcano that was grumbling uneasily. A smaller volcano had erupted right on the edge of the settlement. By the worst possible luck this was the one point that could endanger the islanders since there was no place on the island for them to shelter.

There was only one thing for it. They launched their longboats with the few precious portable possessions they could carry in safety and took to the sea, leaving their cottage homes and furniture to the mercy of the Atlantic gales and the worst that the lava flow from the volcano could do. They steered for Nightingale Island, thirty-seven kilometres away, and all made it in safety. Eventually a British ship picked up their distress signals and was able to rescue them and bring them to England.

In the event, the volcano was not as destructive as it appeared to be when it erupted. When an advance party of six men went to Tristan a year later they found that the main lava flow had missed the village and had poured into the sea, but it had changed the contours of the island slightly. It left blue-black walls of cooled lava, twenty metres high, close to the village.

The volcano that erupted on Tristan da Cunha in 1961

The main body of the islanders returned to their homes in April 1963 to live in the shadow of the volcano. Fishing is the mainstay of the Tristans. They have a small but well-organised and flourishing crayfish industry owned by a South African company. But that small volcano changed more than the geographical features of the island. To some extent it changed the islanders' outlook on life and their ways. In Britain they had been exposed to bright lights, bingo halls, shops, cinemas and television. Their return to the lonely little island meant a severe period of read-justment. A few never made their homes on the island again. They didn't want to. Life in Britain had spoiled it for them. But for those who returned there is always the threat of another eruption.

How those people came to live on Tristan in the first place is a strange story. British seamen occupied the island at the beginning of the nineteenth century during the Napoleonic wars. They landed to make sure the French did not use it as a base to rescue the Emperor Napoleon, who had been banished to the island of St Helena more than 1,600 kilo-

A Tristan and his donkey

metres north of Tristan. When the seamen left, after the danger of such a rescue had passed, one man named William Glass asked to be allowed to stay on Tristan to guard the stores. Later, several shipwrecked sailors joined him, and finally some women came from St Helena and a community sprang up. At present there are something like forty-two people named Glass on the island.

The Tristans have developed several crafts, such as the carding and spinning of wool from their own sheep, but as craftsmen they really excel in the building of the Tristan longboat, which is beautifully shaped and stoutly constructed with a canvas cover stretched tightly over the hull. This makes it surprisingly durable against the hammering of the Atlantic surf. These longboats, owned by the families or groups that built them, are never used, as they once were, for everyday fishing. They are kept mainly for ceremonial voyages, the yearly trips to Nightingale Island.

In the old days these hazardous annual voyages to a steep and rocky island like Nightingale were made to collect young sea birds to boil down for cooking fat. Today the

A Tristan house

islanders can buy cooking fat in the village store, but they still make their trips and they still gather young shearwaters and albatross for winter supplies of cooking fat and meat. But today it is more of an annual holiday, a re-statement of the islanders' mastery over the island and the sea. The crews stay a fortnight, living in the crude, wooden huts that gave shelter on the night of the volcano.

The islanders are only after young birds. In three expeditions during a summer they collect some 12,000 albatross and shearwater chicks which give each Tristan about 36 litres of free fat. This number makes no serious inroads into the bird population.

More than *one and a half million* great shearwaters nest in burrows on Nightingale Island. It is almost the species' only breeding colony. They nest from January to March, and after breeding they fly north. In the early summer many of them are seen at sea off Newfoundland. Then they head

Building a traditional long boat

towards Greenland. By the end of the summer they are massing over the South Atlantic for the return flight to Tristan. It is likely that the great shearwater, living practically all its life at sea, follows its food — plankton, fish and squid — with the ocean's currents. Plankton, millions and millions of tiny, drifting organisms, are the lowest link in the food chain on which all creatures in the sea depend.

Tristan's albatrosses are one of the smallest of the world's thirteen species. They are the yellow-nosed variety and have a wing span of between 1.8 and 2.4 metres. They nest on Tristan, 600 metres up amid giant ferns. It's windy up there, which is partly why the birds choose this nesting site, because an albatross finds it almost impossible to take off without a good, strong headwind. It's the reason too, why albatrosses occur only in the southern oceans of the world. They know they can rely on the constant strong winds that blow there, not only for the take-off but also for soaring over the waves once they are airborne.

Great shearwaters

12
DEATHTRAP LAKE

When we pause to think about the problem of the survival of wildlife in the world it is easy to blame man for every catastrophe, but this wouldn't be entirely just. In recent years man has had his successes in helping wildlife to survive. Some are known, many are unpublicised. Some are emergency operations in the event of a sudden wildlife crisis, some are carefully planned operations to safeguard a threatened species.

An example of quick reaction to a wildlife emergency was a successful attempt in 1962 to save the lives of more than 100,000 young flamingoes. It was a crisis that had all the urgency and drama of a major news story and it was also about ordinary people helping to save wildlife. The crisis

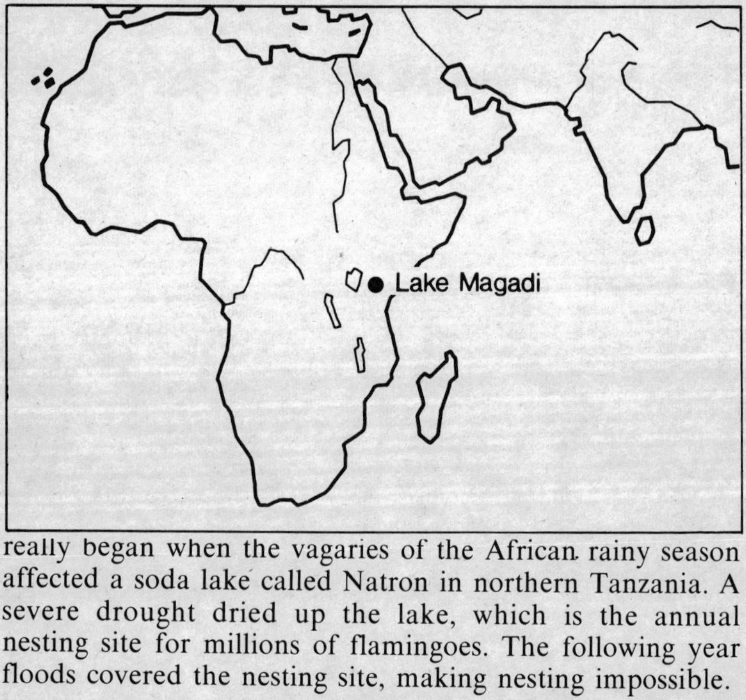

really began when the vagaries of the African rainy season affected a soda lake called Natron in northern Tanzania. A severe drought dried up the lake, which is the annual nesting site for millions of flamingoes. The following year floods covered the nesting site, making nesting impossible.

Lesser flamingo and chick

Driven by the instinct to breed, the flamingoes turned to another soda lake north of Natron called Lake Magadi, just over the border in Kenya. Flamingoes choose to live on soda lakes because they are adapted to feed on the algae these lakes produce. Where such lakes have inaccessible soda flats, they find ideal breeding conditions free from disturbance. With Natron closed to them by drought conditions, Magadi looked tempting.

Magadi is no one's idea of paradise except, perhaps, to a flamingo and even this turned out not to be true. The lake is almost solid soda. It makes soda faster than the dredgers of the Magadi Soda Company can dig it out. This soda concentration was the trap waiting for the nesting flamingoes. More than a million Lesser flamingoes and thousands of Greaters packed the flats there and started to build their cone-shaped nests of soda. It was the first time in living memory they had decided to breed on Magadi. Soon, they were to discover their mistake.

Wildlife film-makers Alan and Joan Root had been watching this spectacular sight with deep interest and delight. Then one evening, soon after the young had begun to hatch, Joan made a discovery that was a warning of the coming tragedy: she found a dead chick. When she picked it up she found it had been blinded — soda splashes had hardened and encased its eyes. More than this — walking through the slushy soda, the frail, stick-like legs had picked up anklets of soda, which had hardened under the hot rays of the sun into crippling leg rings. Weighed down with these, a chick was sure to drown or starve to death. It wasn't happening to the adult birds, who never stood still long enough for the anklets to form.

Alan and Joan Root realised this would be a race against time. Soon, hundreds of thousands of chicks would hatch out. Were they all to die in this miserable way? Help and action came from many sides. Conservationists, industrialists and ordinary people stepped in to help. The soda anklets could be washed off with fresh water but the transport and equipment needed meant money. Within hours, money was

Rescued flamingo chick

Joan Root with soda-encrusted flamingo chick

being collected by the East African Wildlife Society and the World Wildlife Fund. Within days, money was coming from other parts of the world as news of the disaster spread. Even the army sent in a volunteer team to help.

Events moved rapidly at Magadi. Thousands of chicks died quickly and scavengers like Marabou storks moved in to clear up the corpses. But the rescuers — men, women and children — battled on. The fresh-water treatment gave way to a quicker method: sharp hammer blows to shatter the brittle anklets speeded up the rescue.

In all, the operation lasted about twenty-one days. Something like 120,000 chicks were saved from a horrible death. After being freed from their soda anklets they were herded into parts of the lake where the soda concentration was less intense. The rescuers, blistered and soda-burned, could take a well-earned rest.

13
SOS RHINO

Planned rescues of threatened animals have now become an important part of conservation, especially in Africa. These rescues are organised by experts who round up a breeding stock and remove them to a National Park or to an area where they will be able to breed in safety. The modern method of capture is to shoot a dart loaded with an immobilising drug called M99 into an animal, place it in a stockade while it is helpless, bring it round with a tranquiliser, and then let it settle down for a few weeks in its new surroundings before transporting it, sometimes by road, sometimes by air, to the area chosen for release.

Sometimes an animal is located by helicopter and the dart shot from the air. Sometimes, it is stalked on foot or from

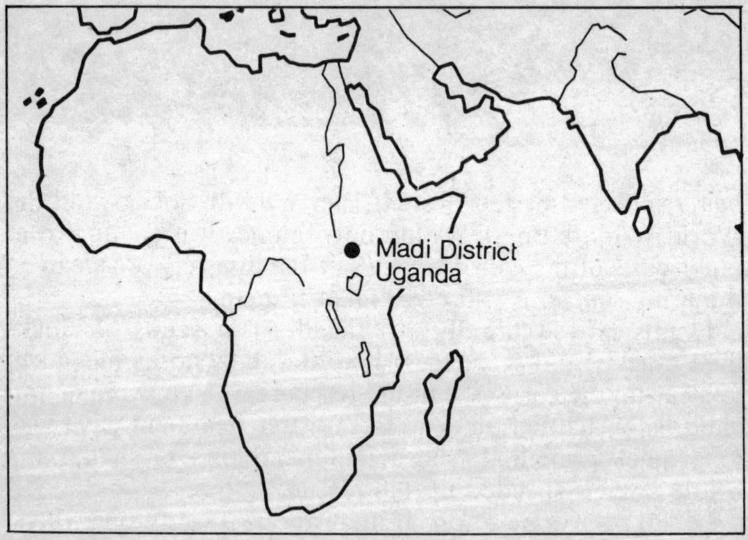

a Land Rover — the method depends largely on the kind of country in which the animal lives.

One of the first mass rescues of wild animals occurred in the early 1960s when white rhino were moved from Madi District in West Nile, Uganda, to Murchison Falls National

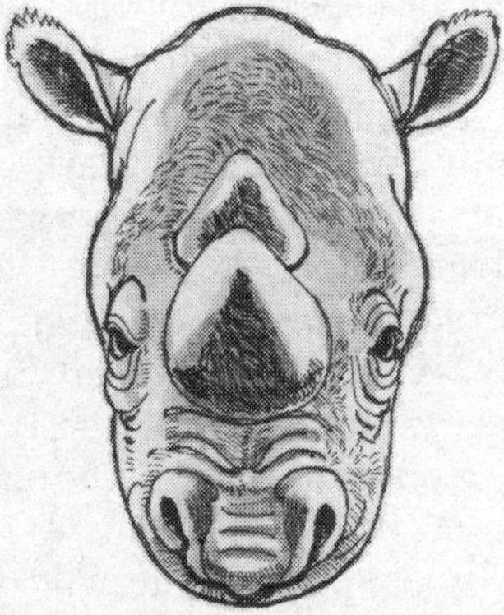

Black rhino

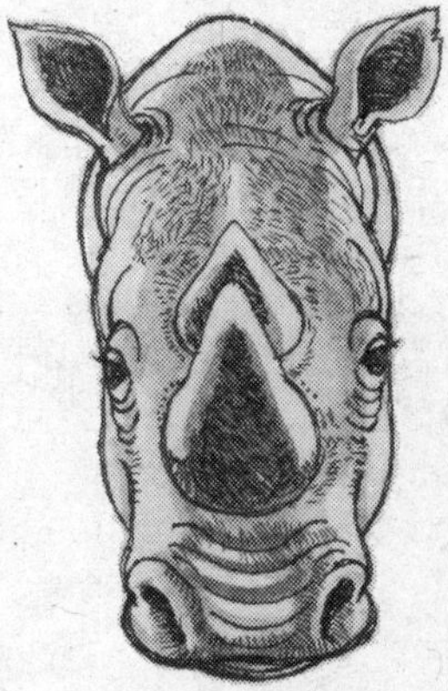

White or wide-mouthed rhino

Park. At that time Madi District contained practically the last of these animals in Uganda. White rhinos are not white. The term comes from an Afrikaans word 'wijd' meaning wide, because these animals have broad, square-lipped mouths, one of the features that distinguishes them from black rhino.

In the 1920s the total number remaining on earth had sunk to a few hundred. They had been hunted, shot and poached because of a superstition in Far Eastern countries that rhino horn, ground to powder, produced a love potion.

When it was decided to move the white rhino one vital problem presented itself: how were these animals, the second largest land animals on earth (next to the elephant), to be caught? The method of firing an anaesthetic dart was then in its infancy. It had been successfully used on other animals — but not yet on the white rhino. Scientists had found that other drugs used safely on certain big game animals were quite likely to kill the rhinos, so it was decided to lasso the three-ton beasts. The Uganda National Parks hired an experienced team of animal catchers — Ken Randall and Pat O'Connell; Colin Willock, head of the

Survival unit, joined in the operation. He says: 'The sight of a three-tonne rhino bashing the daylights out of the flimsy catching-truck in which we were operating was something I will never forget. But the catchers knew their job and, in the end, we successfully caught and transported twenty white rhino to the Park.' As a result of this rescue operation the chances of this magnificant animal surviving was guaranteed in Uganda. In the Murchison Falls National Park they could graze and live in the same wild conditions with one important advantage — safety from poachers.

Meantime, far south in the Umfolozi and Hluhluwe Game Parks of Natal in South Africa, a quite different situation existed. By careful conservation methods, the Parks there had managed to build up a surplus of these animals, at least 1,500 of them. So it seemed right that some of this surplus should be sent to other areas, both in the wild and in zoos.

Perhaps the boldest decision was to set up a breeding herd of forty white rhinos at Whipsnade Zoo in England. Then if anything happened to white rhinos in the wild, the future of the species could be assured and wild areas restocked when conditions were right.

Roping a white rhino. Nowadays drugs are used

A white rhino en route to Whipsnade

This time the rhinos were caught by the improved darting technique. By now the Natal Parks had had so much practice that the time taken from darting to crating was just forty minutes — a far cry from the early days of lassoing.

When the 8,000-tonnes freighter *Kinnaird Castle* set sail

White rhino grazing at Whipsnade

from South Africa bound for England her cargo consisted of canned fruit, hardboard, asbestos, copper — and twenty white rhinos destined to live out their lives in the green fields of Bedfordshire.

White rhinos are grazing animals and at Whipsnade the introduced herd spend the summer outside in an enclosure of some twelve hectares. This is a potato patch if you compare it with the kilometres of space in their former African home. But the rhinos have everything they need at Whipsnade and the proof is that they have already started to breed. In winter the animals are provided with a big house and food — about 12 kilos of concentrates (which includes oats, bran and maize) and 27 kilos of hay a day for one adult rhino.

Whipsnade has an excellent record for breeding animals in captivity. Eighty per cent of all their animals were born there, an achievement that gives us a comforting feeling that if some major disaster were to strike down every white rhino left in Africa those that travelled the long, long way from Umfolozi are safe here.

14
FIRST CATCH YOUR UNICORN

One large and beautiful antelope that manages to live on the fringes of the merciless Namib desert in South West Africa is the gemsbok, the southern race of oryx. This superbly muscled animal has twin, needle-sharp horns stabbing straight upwards from the top of the head. It is believed that in ancient times people mistook the gemsbok or oryx for the unicorn, and it is true that if you catch sight of one in profile at a distance it appears to be a one-horned creature.

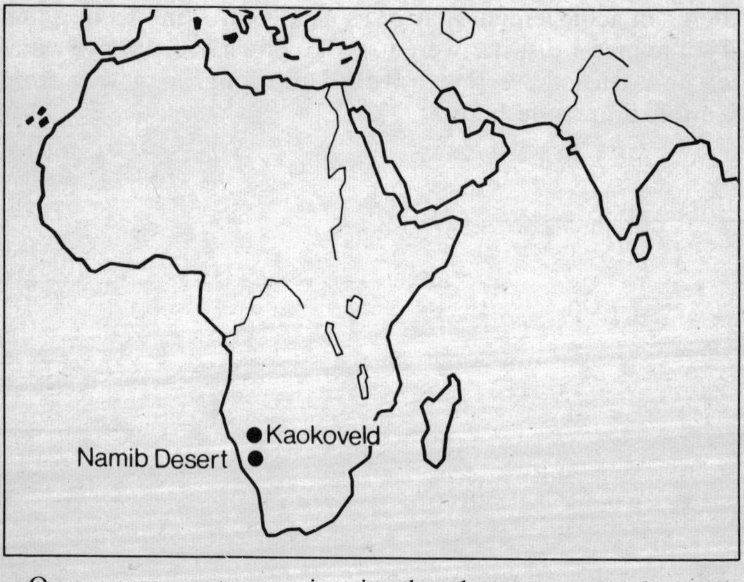

Oryx manage to survive in the desert extremely well. They can go longer than a camel without water. They lick the dew and condensed droplets of water from the scrub and they graze off tough, sparse desert grass. But sometimes, very naturally, herds of oryx migrate to where the living is a bit easier, such as the sheep-farming lands, for pasture and water. A farmer who has to think of the needs of thousands of valuable Karakul sheep (the wool of the Karakul can end up as a £4,000 Persian lamb coat) is likely to reach for his gun when the oryx show up.

When it's wild animal against armed man the animal loses every time. Sometimes, as here, there can be a compromise, another solution. So the South West Africa Conservation Department decided to round up some oryx and transport them by truck to a safer area, far away from the temptation of sheep farms. A herd was chased at 64 kilometres an hour by men in stripped-down Land Rovers with a protective framework for them to hold on to, zooming over sand dunes, tearing along the flat, twisting and turning in clouds of dust and sand.

The catcher, perched on the front wing of the truck, seized an animal by the tail in full flight and wrestled it to a standstill, knowing that one mistake could mean being impaled on those sabre-like horns.

After the oryx were caught, each one was given a shot of tranquillising drug and then taken to a screened holding pen

Catching gemsbok in the Namib desert

to allow it to recover from the shock. They were kept there at least a week before being moved to the Etosha National Park where they could settle down in safety and breed.

You may wonder why they had to catch an oryx by the tail in the middle of the desert. These animals have enormous reserves of strength. If they had been darted with a drug they could have escaped into the 300-metre-high sand dunes where no vehicles could follow. There they might have died before the men, who had come to save them, could inject the vital antidote that brings a drugged animal round again.

Darting is the most effective way of capturing alive any wild animal, although techniques and dosages are different for different-sized animals. Moving animals often requires different methods because their temperament and size must be taken into consideration, as well as the kind of country across which they have to be transported. In South West Africa two species of antelope that urgently needed to be moved to safety recently were the black-faced impala and the roan.

The gemsbok is ready to be transported. Those horns can kill a lion

The world's last few herds of black-faced impala exist in a tribal area of South West Africa called the Kaokoveld, 480 kilometres from the Etosha National Park. For a large part of the year the land in this tribal area is dry and the river beds are waterless. Many animals — and not all of them wild — compete for the sparse grazing. A tribe called the Ovahimbos graze their goats and cattle in what is, after all, their homeland. They take what little water there is during the dry season. Driven away from the water holes, extinction faced these last herds of black-faced impala. Then the Conservation Department capture unit moved in. The impala were so shy and highly strung that the capture unit had to work at night using spotlights (all attempts to drive the animals into nets in daylight had failed. At night, however, the lights tended to confuse the impala so that they could be chased on foot and seized by the horns.

The terrain in the Kaokoveld is so rough that it would have taken days to transport the catch to Etosha by lorry. By then the animals might have died, so the South African Air Force supplied a Dakota aircraft. Suitably tranquillised and cooled by vets sprinkling water over them, the impala made the trip successfully, roped down to the floor of the aircraft. They are now thriving in their new home.

Another rescue operation, this time of roan antelope, called for the combined air power of a helicopter and a twenty-tonne, one-million-pound, four-engined Hercules transport plane.

Roan are the biggest and most powerful of antelopes. Tough and very aggressive, they needed the most careful treatment after they had been darted. Even under drugs any spasmodic movement of the head with those scimitar horns would be dangerous to a handler, and they would certainly not have stood up to the long, bumpy journey in lorries to Etosha across some of the roughest country in Africa. It was decided to use the helicopter for the darting and the Hercules to carry the animals to Etosha in one big airlift.

Manoeuvring a helicopter close to fast-moving animals is a highly specialised job and it needed a 'gunner' with a very good eye to aim those darts. The pilot of the Hercules had

A roan antelope coming round after being darted

his problems too. The only runway available for landing and te-off with a full load was the dried-up bed of a river.

The helicopter was flown by an ex-RAF squadron leader. The dart gunner was a South West African Conservation Department veterinary surgeon, a specialist in darting technique. First, the helicopter had to search out the herds, which usually number about twenty or thirty. A roan antelope can be very tricky to catch up with. It can turn in its own length and twist into a change of direction like lightning. It is capable of bursts of 48 kilometres per hour across an open plain. For the helicopter pilot the operation meant hazardous low-level flying, with one eye on possible obstructions ahead, the other on the speeding animal, and striving to zoom close enough for the marksman to get his dart in. And when a dart struck home the helicopter still had to follow the antelope because it ran a considerable

Roan awaiting airlift to Etosha National Park

distance before the action of the drug brought it to a standstill. The helicopter then radioed a pick-up truck and the antelope was taken to a holding pen to rest and recover.

The next stage was to get seventy-four frightened antelope organised for the mass flight. They could not be allowed to stampede all over the big transport plane during the flight, so they were given just enough drug to keep them docile. They were put aboard on loading pallets packed with soft sawdust; cargo nets were used to make sure that if one or two threw off the effects of the drug more quickly than the others, they would still be under control. Finally, as an additional precaution, the horns of some of the bigger animals were loosely tied in such a way that they could move their heads freely and yet not cause any damage with their horns. Vets were on board to keep watch during the flight.

Just after dawn the thunderous take-off of the big Hercules with only about 64 metres of river bed runway to spare was accomplished. The slightest miscalculation on the part of the pilot and the whole load would have crashed. As it was the plane arrived at Etosha for a big welcome. For the roan antelope it meant not only a welcome — it meant that its kind was no longer threatened with total extinction. It had a future in a National Park.

15
WINGS OVER THE RIFT

The more man learns about other living creatures that share the earth with him, the more efficiently will he be able to control and preserve them.

Dr Colin Pennycuick is an expert on bird flight. Recently, when he went to lecture at Nairobi University, he had an ideal opportunity to study vultures and their place in the wildlife pattern of Africa. Vultures spend much of their time soaring over the plains searching for food. So Dr Pennycuick decided that the only way to study them was to fly like them. Fortunately, he is not only an authority on bird flight, he is also an expert glider pilot.

To help him in this work Anglia Television and Dr Bernhard Grzimek (who in addition to being Director of

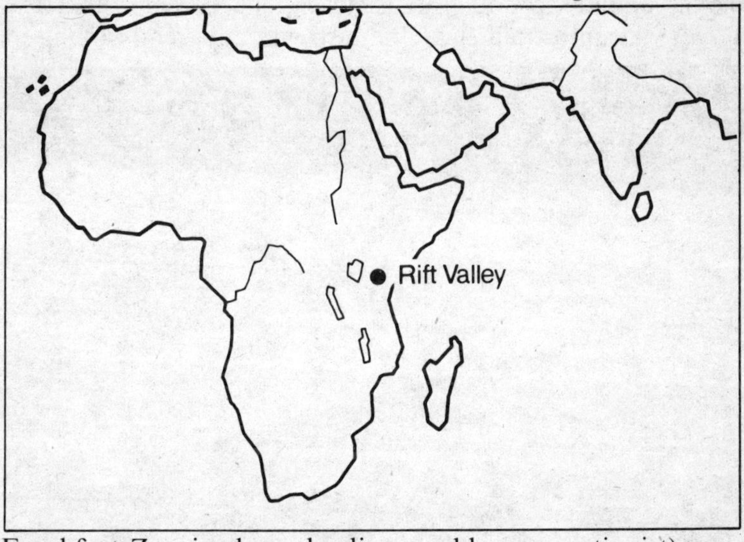

Frankfurt Zoo is also a leading world conservationist) presented him with a special machine. It was a high-performance German sailplane, a Schleicher Ask 14. It is a very special sailplane because it is equipped with a lightweight engine, just powerful enough to allow it to take off

and cruise under power until the pilot decides to switch off the engine, feather the propeller and glide. After a run of only about 90 metres on its single-wheel undercarriage, the Ask 14 can become airborne from any level strip in the bush. This was important since there are few ready-made airstrips in the African bush.

Vultures are not a threatened species but we know very little about them. For instance: how do they find the dead animals on which they feed as scavengers? Is it a combination of sight and smell? Do they watch the flight behaviour of other vultures who have sighted a kill? How far do they range for food? How efficient are they as flying machines? These were some of the questions Dr Pennycuick hoped to answer.

An amazing new discovery about one species of vulture had been made. In the late 1960s, in the same part of the Rift Valley, film naturalists Jane and Hugo van Lawick noticed some Egyptian vultures apparently throwing large stones on the ground. But a closer look revealed that the target was an ostrich egg. One bird was apparently trying to

Dr Pennycuick and Masai tribesmen beside the powered glider

crack it. Later, the whole amazing process was captured on film. One vulture tried to break open the ostrich egg with its beak and failed. Another vulture came along, picked up a large stone in its beak and slammed it down on the ground. After doing this a few times, the bird scored a direct hit on the egg, cracking the shell so that it could get at the meat inside. No one knows whether this remarkable piece of animal behaviour has been going on for years or is newly learned.

The species Dr Pennycuick intended to study was one of the largest in Africa, Ruppell's griffon vulture. If the griffon is awkward and repulsive on the ground, it is graceful and beautiful in flight. Both vulture and sailplane have a good deal in common. Both rely on rising columns of warm air called thermals. The vulture, it seems, feels them instinctively and by flying wingtip to wingtip with these birds, Dr Pennycuick studied how they used the thermals in the search for food. For instance, the griffon displays one feature that aircraft designers have copied — slots that smooth out the airflow and prevent both a plane and the

griffon from stalling at low speeds. But the slotted wingtip feathers of the griffon, stretched out like human fingers, are more effective than anything man has invented. The vulture's wingtip feathers not only smooth out the airflow — they actually twist in flight, acting as little propellers giving forward power.

Dr Pennycuick has discovered that there are occasions when vultures have difficulty in flying and sometimes cannot fly at all! There is a relationship between the power of the body muscles required to fly and the body weight. Larger vultures, storks and pelicans would hardly be able to stay airborne but for this ability to extract energy from the atmosphere and use it as an aid to flying.

Early in the morning on the East African plains it is possible to see groups of vultures that have gathered at some carcase the night before and slept there. If they are chased they will take off, but then fly only a few metres. If they are chased continually and thus have to take off several times, they become exhausted very quickly and can be caught by hand. The Ruppell's griffon vulture and the white-backed

vulture can be caught in this way. Later in the morning, when the thermals are stronger and the birds are less heavy with food they can take off when chased and climb in tight circles. Dr Pennycuick found that the best soaring time of the day was usually between 11 a.m. and 4 p.m.

There are several kinds of lift. For instance, there is the slope lift in which the air rises when the wind meets the slope of a hill or mountain. Soaring birds learn to locate currents like these and use them. Dr Pennycuick observed that as soon as one vulture was climbing successfully, others joined it, circling round the very centre of a thermal where the lift is strongest.

There are times when the vultures can beat man at flying despite all our knowledge of aerodynamics. Early in the day, when the thermals tend to be weak and narrow, the vulture often outclimbs the glider because it can turn in much smaller circles. The glider, being bigger and unable to make such tight turns, cannot get the same benefit from the narrow up-draught. On one occasion Dr Pennycuick found himself being outclimbed by a tawny eagle, even though he

A white-backed vulture

had his engine working while the eagle was only gliding.

Vultures need to arrive quickly at the spot where there is a dead animal so, by climbing in thermals and gliding in different directions, they keep up a patrol over a wide area. It has an advantage over a scavenger animal like the hyena who reacts to activity in the distance but has to travel across country on four legs to get to the dead animal.

Dr Pennycuick found that Ruppell's griffon, which nests in colonies on cliffs, travelled further than any other for food. It will forage some 160 kilometres from thc nesting area to get food to bring back to its young.

Vultures perching in tree above kill

16
THE FAMILY THAT LIVED WITH ELEPHANTS

African elephants are terribly destructive to trees. They eat the leaves and bark of many varieties, especially the many species of acacia. They will rip off the branches to get at the leaves. In the dry season they shake the acacias to release a golden rain of seed pods (sometimes uprooting the tree) picking up the pods delicately with their trunks and throwing them into their mouths. To get at the bark, they gouge the tree with their tusks and then rip off the bark — which ensures that the tree will die. The seed pods they deposit in their droppings often take root, but a tree takes a long time to grow.

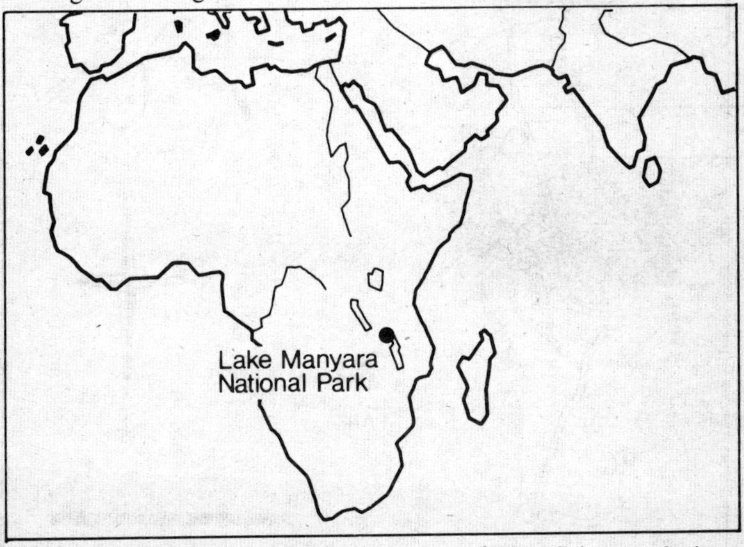

No one knows precisely how much land is needed to support an elephant. Different environments of Africa mean different problems, but one general estimate is about three elephants to 260 hectares.

Lake Manyara National Park in Tanzania stretches for 48

kilometres along the lake shore and nowhere is it more than 6 kilometres wide. It lies between a steep wall of the Rift Valley and the lake itself. To the north are banana planta-

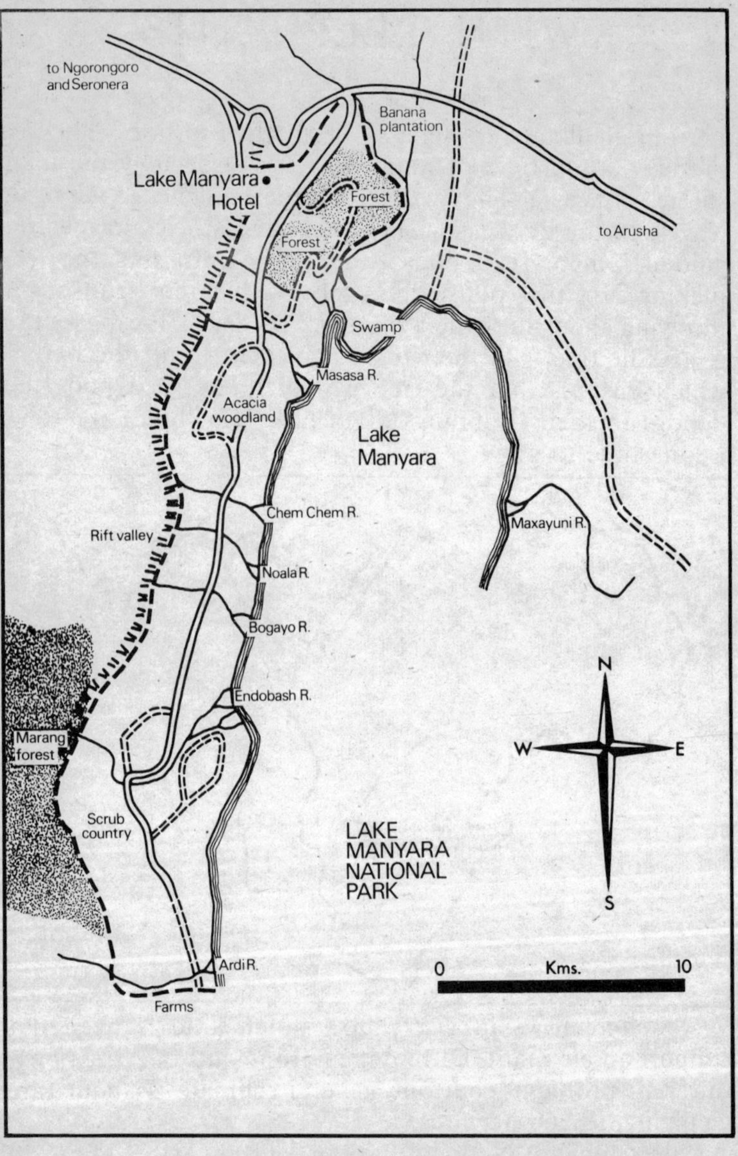

tions. To the south, farms. In places to the west the buttresses of the Rift walls stretch right down to the lake shore. At the highest point the rim is nearly 300 metres above the lake. At the top of this escarpment lie 23,400 hectares of the Marang Forest Reserve — outside the National Park and therefore denied to the elephants.

In the boundaries of the Park itself 500 elephants live, the densest population in Africa, over twelve to 260 hectares. It has been estimated that at the present rate of destruction the acacia woodlands will be exhausted by 1980.

A young Scottish scientist, Dr Iain Douglas-Hamilton with his wife and two small daughters lived among the Manyara elephants for five years while he studied them. There were too many elephants in too small a space, and his task was to find out for the Tanzania National Parks how the elephants could continue to exist in balance with their environment. He was absolutely determined about one thing: he would not kill a single elephant to further his research. He approached his problem in another way. He decided to get to know every elephant, its family history and its relationship with the rest of the group.

With the aid of a grant from the New York Zoological Society he built a Robinson Crusoe kind of house in the Park. Constructed from local stone, timber and reeds it stood at a spot above the river Ndala, where elephants could often be observed when they came to drink and bathe, and it was here that the Douglas-Hamiltons were to live for five years.

Concentrating on the elephant families one by one, Iain gradually built up a file of the personal details of every elephant. In the file were individual identity photographs, a record of each animal's actions observed by Iain, and details like tusk shapes and any kind of special markings or colouring. At first he gave each elephant a number, but he abandoned that system because he found it easier to remember them by naming them. The names he chose were sometimes based on some physical feature of the animal, such as 'Broken Tusk', but more often, he used a name famous in history or stories — Boadicea, Ariadne, Virgo, Catherine the Great and Diana.

Baby elephant stripping bark from acacia tree

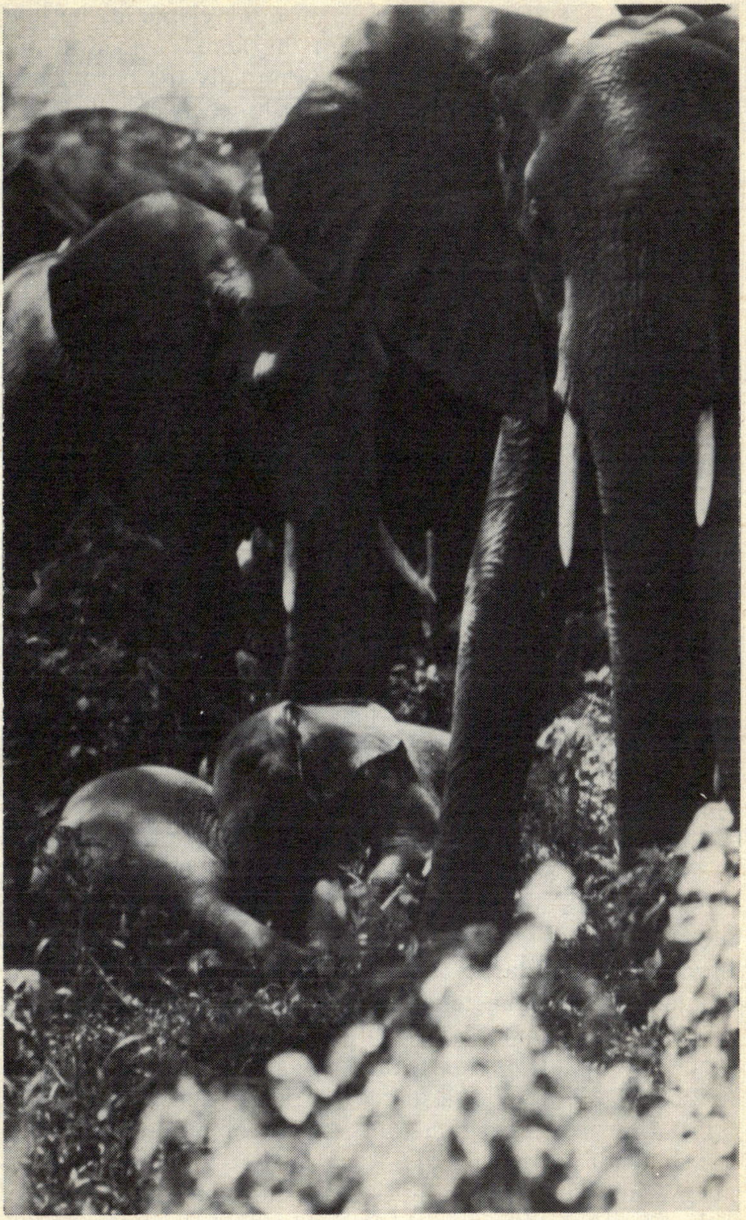

Elephant young being shaded from the sun

Once he got to know and recognise the elephants he had to learn their ages, particularly of the females, to find out how often they had young and how rapidly the herds were increasing. There is a direct relationship between shoulder height and age and he was able to find this out by taking photographs with a device like a range finder; this gave a double image from which the height could be worked out.

He followed the wanderings of each elephant family, studying their behaviour. He got to know the personalities and temperaments of the creatures. He learned to move about among these lethal animals on foot — something that anyone else would be ill-advised to do in the bush.

He had several narrow escapes, notably from four sisters he called the Torone gang, which sounds like something out of an old gangster movie. All had savage records. Torone number one charged his Land Rover, slamming her tusks through the radiator. Torone number two savaged a tourist's minibus. Torone number three charged another Land Rover and Torone number four had to be shot in self-defence by a Park ranger when she attacked a visitor's car. There are only a few violent elephants and Iain never blamed the Torone gang. In fact, he sympathised with them. He felt sure that at some time they had been shot at and possibly wounded, perhaps by poachers or while raiding farmland for food. A banana plantation or a maize crop is a big temptation for an elephant.

Elephant society is ruled by the females. The leader of each group is a female. And it was Iain's encounters with these nervous, and sometimes fierce, matriarchs that were the most nerve-racking. Boadicea was a typical matriarch, the leader of a large family of twenty-two animals. She would always make terrifying threat charges, which were, more often than not, sheer bluff. All the younger females looked to Boadicea for leadership and two other families tended to follow at a distance, forming what Iain called a 'kinship group'. At siesta time the junior mothers stood in the shade of a tree with their own calves while Boadicea was always in a flank position on watchful guard. Any kind of a threat and the cows would form a defensive circle with the young in the centre.

Boadicea charges

Iain made a very important discovery about the organisation of the elephant family. He found that there was a sharp difference between the life of the male elephant calf and that of the female calf. When they are very young they are protected equally but as they grow older the young bulls, who soon begin play-fighting, are kept strictly in their place. Then, when a bull is about thirteen years of age and begins to worry the female calves, the matriarchs decide it is time for it to leave the family circle. The young bull is forcibly driven out. But it will hang around the family for a few years, keeping its distance, perhaps a kilometre away. From then on it lives the life of a bachelor. In fiction stories it is always the bull elephants who are the rogues. In fact, the bachelor bulls are very mild compared to the matriarchs.

After being expelled from the family, the bull gradually learns its place in male society by play-fighting with the other bulls it meets on its wanderings. When it is grown to full stature it will be accepted by the matriarch of another family to mate with a young female, but after that the separation of the two sexes is once again maintained.

Two young bull elephants play-fighting

Iain found that all the elephants in Manyara knew each other well. When two families approached each other, the youngsters would often run across and intermingle. He discovered that although Manyara has the highest population density in Africa it also has a healthy breeding rate with a high proportion of young — at least, while the woodlands last. But if the woods go, the elephant population will quickly suffer a fatal decline.

Iain also wanted to find out how family groups moved over long periods. To do this he had to place small radio transmitters on selected, newly expelled young bulls that were loosely attached to their families. As the bull wandered it would send out a bleep-bleep signal that could be picked up over a range of 48 kilometres. Then, flying his own plane from a bush airstrip near his camp, Iain was able to track selected bulls and, in this way, trace the seasonal movements of certain family units.

At the end of the experiment he had an accurate picture of how individual groups moved in search of food throughout the year. He learned how they headed for the Marang forest on top of the southern escarpment during the dry season in search of food. Unfortunately, the routes to this were largely blocked by farmlands. He found, too, that the elephants used the dense forest at the northern end, close to the banana plantations. Bananas are a favourite elephant delicacy, so stopping their raids on the plantations became a matter of urgency. Iain's answer was an electrified fence. It worked. Elephants are quick to learn from an unpleasant experience. After receiving a mild shock they never went near the fence again.

The most significant single fact revealed by this radio-tracking study was how urgently the elephants needed access to the extra food in the Marang forest especially when the Park below dried up before the rains came. As a result of the study, the Marang forest has now been added to the Park area by the Tanzanian Government. So the elephants of Manyara look as though they have an excellent chance of survival at last.

But before all this was accomplished, however, Iain had his narrowest escape of all. It happened when he tried to get one of his two radio transmitters back from a bull that had been driven out of a family group ruled over by an enormous matriarch called Sarah. The bull seemed a safe distance away from Sarah's family when Iain fired a dart loaded with drug. Unfortunately, the bull trumpeted in alarm as the dart struck. Immediately, Sarah appeared screaming in fury and, to add to the terror of the spectacle, there were three or four angry matriarchs with her. Iain knew he had to get an antidote into the drugged bull if it wasn't to suffer permanent damage from the original dart, but he didn't have another dart with which to administer the antidote. Sarah would kill him for certain if he tried to approach the bull on foot and inject the antidote — but this seemed to be the only choice.

Then an incredible thing happened in this battle of wits. Sarah and the other cows in the family group tried to raise the drugged two-tonne elephant to its feet with their tusks. Only a man who loves elephants could have done what Iain did next. After making several attempts to approach on foot and being charged by Sarah, he got into his Land Rover, drove at full speed straight towards the group of furious elephants, leaned over the side and plunged the needle, with the vital antidote, into the bull.

Instantly, Sarah charged and this time her tusks smashed into the front of the Land Rover, squashing the steering wheel and missing Iain's head by centimetres. He threw himself backwards so violently to avoid them that he broke the back of the seat. All this time, Sarah was pushing the vehicle backwards at 32 kilometres per hour until finally it smashed into a tree. Now Sarah was satisfied and backed off. The enemy on wheels had been dealt with and the bull was beginning to come round none the worse for wear. Iain was satisfied too. He had succeeded in saving the bull although he had come close to losing his own life. The Land Rover was virtually a write-off.

One of the most moving experiences during Iain's work was when he watched Boadicea's family come across the bones of dead elephants shot by poachers. They sniffed and touched the bones and carefully gathered them up, sometimes in their mouths, sometimes in their trunks, and carried them short distances away, spreading them around and dropping them out of sight in the undergrowth. There is no explanation for this bone scattering. Sometimes, the elephants bury the bones. Perhaps it was this strange occurrence, observed by early hunters, that gave rise to the belief that elephants went to secret places to die, mysterious, hidden places that held a priceless treasure of ivory.

Iain and his family will never forget the Manyara elephants. Probably the most touching thing that ever happened to him was when, after a two-year interval of work back at Oxford, he returned to Manyara. Virgo, a one-tusked elephant, recognised and greeted him. It was a cautious advance on both sides until Virgo placed the tip of her trunk into Iain's outstretched hand. Then, some days later, she brought her two calves out of the bush to greet Iain.

Oria Douglas-Hamilton and her two children watch wild elephant group

17
THE ENCHANTED ISLES

The Galapagos Islands are a small group 960 kilometres out in the Pacific ocean, west of Ecuador in South America. They are acknowledged as being very important to the world by all naturalists — but why? The answer is in their unique history. The Galapagos exploded out of the bed of the sea only two or three million years ago — many, many millions of years after the other land masses of this earth had cooled. Much of the blue-black lava of the islands looks almost freshly cooled. It is still unweathered and razor sharp. On the coasts, the sea has broken through in places to form sheltered bays.

In the million or so years since the Galapagos were born, the islands have received a slow trickle of small creatures,

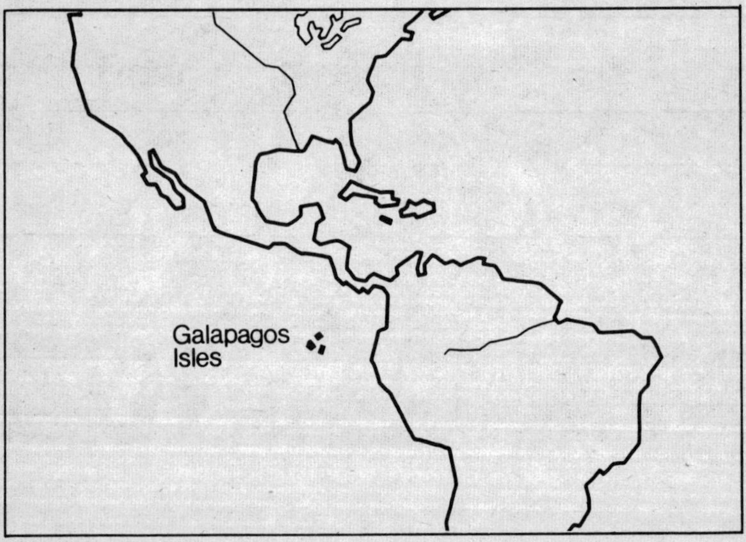

such as spiders and the non-poisonous Galapagos snake, on floating debris carried along on the Humboldt current that sweeps the icy Antarctic waters up the west coast of South America and round the islands.

To set foot on these islands for the first time is to have the strange and thrilling feeling of suddenly moving back millions of years in time. There is still the final, miraculous sensation: all the birds and animals are tame. They have no fear of man. You are surrounded by sea lions, sea birds, iguanas and mocking thrushes, few of whom bother to fly or move away.

In the brief four hundred years since man first found the islands, wildlife suffered terribly at the hands of pirates, marauders and seal hunters. The event that put the islands on the navigation charts occurred in 1535 when the Bishop of Panama was blown off course while on a mission to Peru and found himself at the Galapagos. Then followed the buccaneers who ran their ships ashore to refit. Pirates pillaged the wildlife for fresh food, particularly the largest animal of the Galapagos, the giant tortoise, weighing some 90 kilos. They took them aboard ship by the thousand to feed their crews. It came close to extinction and even today it is one of the rare species most needing help. Its movements and habits are being carefully studied in the hope that its numbers can be built up

Joan Root tries to cook, pestered by Galapagos mocking birds

Marine iguanas exist nowhere else in the world but in the Galapagos islands

Galapagos sea lion and young

Rats escaped from the ships and established themselves on the islands and the pirates put goats ashore to breed as future stocks of meat. The destructive goats are still there stripping what little vegetation there is.

When Charles Darwin made his voyage to the islands in 1835 aboard H.M.S. *Beagle,* he studied the wildlife, and it was from what he observed there that he got the first clue to the theory of evolution, contained in his book *The Origin of the Species.* It was a theory that turned the Victorian world upside down. Up to that time people believed man, and indeed all animal life, had been created by God exactly as it is today; that no physical progress or change had been made. Darwin's theory was that all life had been gradually modified and had adapted itself to existence in its own particular environment.

He observed that almost every creature on these islands was quite different from its nearest relative, not only in other parts of the world, but on other islands within the Galapagos group. It became apparent to him that these creatures had adapted to local conditions. The land iguanas,

A marine iguana and a swallow-tailed gull

The Galapagos flightless cormorant

for instance, yellowish-orange underneath, brownish-red above, don't occur anywhere else in the world. They are completely different in colouring, shape and habit from the marine iguanas of the Galapagos, the only lizard adapted for feeding on marine vegetation such as algae and seaweed.

Then there are the Galapagos cormorants, which have existed for so long without enemies that they have abandoned flying altogether, so their stubby wings no longer serve any useful purpose. The young cormorants don't have to waste time and energy learning to fly. They are at home in the water, and underwater too.

There are only about 3,000 pairs of Waved albatrosses in the world and they all nest in the dry scrub on Hood Island in the Galapagos. They get their name because their bodies, from the throat down to the chest and underparts, are covered with wavy, close-set lines. They have an extraordinary courtship display, a kind of beak fencing match with a lot of ceremonial bowing interrupted by opening of bills as though giving enormous yawns. There is a strange caricature of a walk and even odder sounds, including one that resembles hysterical laughter.

One of Darwin's main clues came from a group of birds now called Darwin's finches. These birds have developed different-shaped beaks for different ways of getting food. One has a heavy beak for seed cracking, another has a lighter beak for probing seed pods. Originally, they came from the South American mainland, but nature and necessity modified them in this way to make use of the different sources of food once they had arrived in the Galapagos. The woodpecker finch has even learned to use a tool. It breaks off a twig or cactus spine, holds it in its beak and probes out insects from the bark of rotting trees. It has the distinction of being one of the few tool-using animals, a group that includes man.

Why is the wildlife so tame? The instinct of fear takes many thousands of years to develop. The touching, but at the same time tragic, feature of Galapagos wildlife is that there has not been time for fear of man to take root, so the creatures are desperately vulnerable. Fur seals are the exception. They have suffered in the past from wholesale massacre by invading ships' crews. The sealers killed for fur

The woodpecker finch probing for insects using a twig

and profit. Perhaps some instinctive memory of that slaughter still lives on.

We all have a responsibility to see that the creatures of these enchanted isles need never develop the instinct of fear at all. Quite apart from this, the Galapagos are a living laboratory, a demonstration, as Darwin rightly deduced, of evolution in action. With proper conservation and sensible management, these remarkable islands can become one of the most fascinating attractions to the growing number of people all over the world who are interested in natural history.

A start has been made. Modern conservation and management are enabling the islands to attract a growing number of visitors. Now, special cruise liners call there. The tourists they bring are rather special too! They are in properly conducted parties led by wildlife experts. This kind of invasion is welcomed by conservationists because, like everything else, conservation costs money and the tourists help to pay for it.

The heavy seed-eating bill of a Galapagos ground finch

18
NOW OR NEVER

A quiet, peaceful scene by a river bank in Africa, looking exactly like the bank of an English river on a summer morning. The first hint that something unusual is about to happen is when a flock of bright golden birds flies towards the river in an almost empty sky. Then more and more come into view and begin settling by the river until, for a kilometre back, the ground is covered with them. The birds are chestnut-bellied sand grouse, 40,000 of them, and they have flown 30 or 50 kilometres from all around the arid, drought-hit countryside to get a drink of water. For a few minutes the sky is full of a wheeling mass of birds.

It is a picture of total chaos to the human eye — but not to the sand grouse. By watching carefully we discover an order in what appears to be a jumbled mass, a system by which every bird in all those 40,000 drinks its fill. They line up and wait their turn, not like a bus queue, but more like lines of infantry soldiers waiting to go forward. They walk in lines to the water's edge, take eight or nine sips and then fly back to the desert; the birds behind them move up in orderly fashion to take their places.

This whole amazing explosion of life by a tranquil river bank lasts exactly six and a half minutes. It is one of the greatest concentrations of sand grouse ever seen, yet, had it rained the night before, not a single bird would have made that flight to the river.

This is just one tiny incident in the infinite pattern of nature throughout the world. The existence and ways of animals are a constant source of wonder. Does it mean anything to us that scenes in nature like this may disappear permanently?

We have to ask ourselves these basic questions: Do we want wild animals or not? If we do, then it is time we made an effort to do something about it; otherwise, within a critically short period, it will be too late. Time is running out for wild animals and for man.

19
WHAT MAKES A WILDLIFE CAMERAMAN

At this very moment *Survival's* naturalist-cameramen are travelling along dusty African trails, sitting in freezing hides, filming underwater with whales and finding out how gorillas live in the deep rain forest. Some are flying their own aircraft to bring to the TV screens stories such as the ones you have been reading about. Des Bartlett and Dieter Plage are just two who are acknowledged to be among the world's best.

Des Bartlett, an Australian, and his wife Jen, work as a team. He has been filming wildlife for twenty years all over the world. He was born in a town called Tamborine in Queensland where his father was a school teacher.

Des once lived with a tribe of head hunters in Borneo for five months so that he could film them. Jen is an essential part of the team doing all the detailed planning needed for their filming projects.

Dieter Plage is a thirty-five-year-old West German. Part of his boyhood was spent in the horror of war in Nazi Germany. These first years instilled in him a hatred of violence in all its forms. He was nine years old when a group of boys he was going around with found some hand grenades left by retreating soldiers. They threw one into a pond where it exploded, killing most of the fish. To Dieter this was senseless killing; killing just for the sake of killing. With the aid of some friends, who thought the same way that he did, he succeeded in stopping the other boys from throwing any more grenades in the pond.

He was sixteen when his father bought him his first movie camera, and he lost no time filming in the countryside near his home. On leaving school he became a camera assistant in a film studio and when he was twenty he went to South Africa ready to take any job there. In Capetown he worked as a photographic assistant, saving every penny he could for

Ted Eales filming an oystercatcher chick at Blakeney Point

movie equipment. He lived on baked beans for weeks at a time. His next job was in Hollywood working on American films for television. It proved a disappointment. He wanted to hold a camera in his hands and make films, not work on other people's completed films.

Back in South Africa he got his first experience of wildlife filming with an American producer. Finally, Dr Bernhard Grzimek spotted his talent and introduced him to Aubrey Buxton, the producer of *Survival.* Dieter has since made many fine films, learning all about all sorts of animals and places.

But not all cameramen travel thousands of kilometres all over the world for their films. There are some who are experts on the wildlife of Britain and who specialise in making films in this country.

Ted Eales is one. A man with a quiet sense of humour, a fine naturalist and skilled with the camera, he is Warden of Blakeney Point, Norfolk, a National Trust nature reserve famous for its tern colonies in summer and wildfowl in winter. A bleak, flat headland of sand and scrub, Blakeney Point is a natural stopover point for migrating birds and a nesting site for terns. Carried on the north-easterly winds, the birds settle in thousands and in great variety at Blakeney. For many years Ted has watched the cycle of bird life repeating itself on this narrow strip of land.

Blakeney's showpiece is its ternery. Terns are in danger everywhere because people, looking for places to walk, picnic and sunbathe, are invading their nesting beaches and disturbing the nests. To say that terns nest is an exaggeration. They scoop out a shallow hole on the beach and plonk their eggs down there. People are not the only problem. Wind, weather and predators, such as gulls, owls, hedgehogs, rats and stoats, are all enemies of the tern. One year Ted lost 2,000 nests when fierce gales put the whole nesting area under water.

What kind of qualities are needed to become a wildlife cameraman? You must be as fine a film technician as the best feature film cameraman. When I asked Dieter Plage his opinion he said: 'Quite apart from this technical ability, you have to like animals. You have to be physically fit. You

Dieter Plage being chased and nearly killed by bull elephant. His camera lies on the ground.

have to be willing *not* to think in terms of working hours. The moment you begin thinking about Saturdays and Sundays off and of finishing your day at 5.30 p.m. you may as well give up. Wildlife doesn't clock in and clock out.

'A cameraman cannot plan anything in advance where his private life is concerned because he never knows when or where an urgent situation is going to arise. But it is a life with great compensations. No day is like another. Every day offers a new challenge.

'You do not, for instance, walk into the African bush, set up a camera and wait for everything to happen in front of you within twenty minutes. You can ask an actor if he would mind posing by a tree where the light and the background are perfect. Try asking an elephant!'

Dieter talked of the risks that cameramen sometimes choose to take. 'You have to understand the chance you are taking and think the thing through carefully, going over every tiny detail.'

He believes in what has been called 'the smell of fear' and he explained: 'I have found with animals that if you approach them with fear they somehow sense this and I think they smell it. I also believe that if you approach an animal and you think "this awful creature, I hate it" the animal can sense this hostility, although it is impossible to define this scientifically.'

Judgement based on experience is important. 'Experience helps a cameraman to judge what a wild animal is likely to do. Filming lions or elephants, for instance . . . a movement of the ears, a twitch of the tail or some little movement like that will be a warning.'

Cameramen also need a sixth sense when filming in the wild. John Buxton had no thoughts of danger, or any reason to think of it when he went to the North West Territories of Canada to film herds of buffalo. He was dropped by helicopter close to a herd of about 1,000 and took up his camera position behind a huge piece of felled tree. Reasonably safe for anyone you would think. But it is never safe to assume anything where animals are concerned and some sixth sense told him to move from that position — and only just in time.

Rod Borland filming on the 300-metre dunes of the Namib

Suddenly, for no apparent reason, the whole herd stampeded in a thunder of hooves that shook the ground — straight towards that dead tree where John Buxton had been minutes before. He kept his camera going and got great pictures. Had he not moved he would have been steamrollered into the ground by the wildly charging herd. The tree, where he had first taken up his position, was smashed to pieces.

ACKNOWLEDGEMENTS

All the stories in this book are based on the television natural history films produced by *Survival* — Anglia's award-winning television series.

Scientists, naturalists and cameramen are now working in all parts of the world preparing more *Survival* stories, which will be shown on television in the future.

This book could not have been written without the help, experience and wide knowledge of Aubrey Buxton, producer of the series, Colin Willock, head of Anglia's Natural History Unit, Sir Peter Scott, Des Bartlett, Dieter Plage, Sue Harrison and the other men and women, who make up this remarkable team.

Acknowledgements for the photographs

Cover photographs — Des and Jen Bartlett, Alan Root, Don Renn
Wildlife in London — Survival Anglia Ltd
Pelican Flyway — Dieter Plage
The Flight of the Snow Geese — Des and Jen Bartlett
Citizens of the Coral — page 31 - Ben Cropp; page 34 - Valerie Taylor *(Ardea)*
Where Him of the Hairy Hands lives — Don and Kathy Renn; except page 36 - J D Bromhall *(Ardea)*
World of the Beaver — Des and Jen Bartlett
The Trout and the Mayfly — Oxford Scientific Films
The World you never see — Oxford Scientific Films
The Forbidden Desert of the Danakil — Dieter Plage
The Empty Desert — pages 66, 67, 70 - Margit Plage; pages 68, 69 - Rod Borland
The Loneliest Place in the World — George Edwards; except page 73 - Syndication International and page 77 - Dr P Germain *(Ardea)*
Deathtrap Lake — Alan and Joan Root
SOS Rhino — Survival Anglia Ltd
First Catch Your Unicorn — Dieter Plage
Wings over the Rift — Survival Anglia Ltd
The Family that lived with Elephants — Dr Iain Douglas-Hamilton
The Enchanted Isles — Alan Root
What Makes a Wildlife Cameraman — page 122 - Survival Anglia Ltd; page 124 - Bernhard Grzimek Tierbilder/Okapia; page 126 - Rod Borland